C000293731

Praise for *The Four Pill.
Parental Engageme

There will be few teachers and school leaders who do not know the difference that parental engagement makes to both the school environment and the pupils themselves, but how to create a culture of parental engagement has often been shrouded in mystery and left up to luck. In *The Four Pillars of Parental Engagement*, Justin Robbins and Karen Dempster draw upon their own original research and the existing literature to demystify the parental engagement process. They give the reader clear actionable steps as well as an understanding of why these steps matter. I have no doubt that this book will be invaluable to any school seeking the next piece of the school improvement puzzle.

**Mark Enser, research lead and head of geography,
Heathfield Community College, and co-author of *The CPD Curriculum***

Drawing on the voices of parents, pupils and education professionals, this carefully researched book makes a significant contribution to the field of parental engagement. Framing their insights through the four pillars of knowledge, environment, culture and communication, the authors provide a purposeful and practical way for schools to strengthen this aspect of their work. Highly recommended.

Mary Myatt, education writer, speaker and curator of Myatt & Co

The Four Pillars of Parental Engagement is a fantastically useful book. The authors give advice to school leaders and teachers on auditing where they are now, building an effective plan and implementing it successfully. The book fizzes with practical advice, is packed with research findings and contains fascinating insights from wide-ranging case studies. It is a powerful manifesto for investing in building and sustaining impactful parental engagement. As Justin Robbins and Karen Dempster rightly argue, get this right and you will see an impact on pupil performance.

**Rachel Macfarlane, director of education services, Herts for Learning,
and author of *Obstetrics for Schools: A Guide to Eliminating Failure
and Ensuring the Safe Delivery of All Learners***

While we're aware that when home and school work as a team around the child, outcomes are improved – it can nevertheless be hard to know where to start. With their four pillars of parental engagement, the authors give us a framework to scaffold our thinking. They go on to walk us through how to develop and implement a plan, and provide a wide range of case studies and top tips to support its implementation.

The Four Pillars of Parental Engagement is the perfect mix of theory and practice. If you've got parental engagement listed on your school improvement plan, this book will be a blessing.

Dr Pooky Knightsmith, expert on child and adolescent mental health

Insightful, practical and well researched, *The Four Pillars of Parental Engagement* is a must-read for teachers and school leaders alike. Capturing both why communication is important and how to communicate well, the book helps engage us all in the central role that good communication plays in education. The authors' model shapes an exciting vision for genuine parent–pupil–school partnership and recognises that as each part of the trio is responsible and accountable, so each part must have a voice and be heard. Schools who ignore the lessons of this book or don't make time for this discussion in their staffrooms do so at their peril. The revolution in communication is here; we either try to survive it with our heads in the sand or use it to thrive.

This book will be of huge value to schools, teachers, serving and aspiring leaders and even parents, who could better understand how to engage with their school to achieve the best impact for their children.

Chris Wheeler, principal, Monkton Combe School

As we know, parental support is a crucial ingredient in both academic and social success, especially for our most vulnerable students. In *The Four Pillars of Parental Engagement*, Justin Robbins and Karen Dempster set out ways in which schools can build relationships with parents and carers and create a culture of mutual collaboration in order to support all our learners to succeed.

The four pillars at the centre of the book are rooted in extensive research and evidence as to what is effective in engaging parents. They also provide tools for schools to reflect on in their context in order to be able to work towards building a culture of mutual respect, support and collaboration.

This book is essential reading for those who want to build on the opportunities that meaningful relationships with parents can bring for all.

Zoe Enser, author and specialist lead adviser for English

Parental engagement has to be one of the key drivers of success for any school and is so vital, on every level, yet there's surprisingly very little out there to actually help make it happen. In *The Four Pillars of Parental Engagement*, Robbins and Dempster have put together an interesting read that will make you reflect on your school's relationship with your pupils' parents, what works and why, and how we move forward in these changing times. It's a must-read for any senior leader.

Dave McPartlin, head teacher, Flakefleet Primary School

The Four Pillars of Parental Engagement

Empowering schools to connect better with parents and pupils

Justin Robbins and Karen Dempster

independent
thinking press

First published by

Independent Thinking Press
Crown Buildings, Bancyfelin, Carmarthen, Wales, SA33 5ND, UK
www.independentthinkingpress.com

and

Independent Thinking Press
PO Box 2223, Williston, VT 05495, USA
www.crownhousepublishing.com

Independent Thinking Press is an imprint of Crown House Publishing Ltd.

Edited by Ian Gilbert.

British Library Cataloguing-in-Publication Data
A catalogue entry for this book is available from the British Library.

Print ISBN 978-178135395-0
Mobi ISBN 978-178135397-4
ePub ISBN 978-178135398-1
ePDF ISBN 978-178135399-8

LCCN 2021939634

Printed and bound in the UK by
TJ Books, Padstow, Cornwall

Preface

We are passionate about engaging parents to work together with schools so that future generations can be at their best. We believe in it so much that it was the reason we founded Fit2Communicate in 2015.

As parents of school-aged children at various stages of their lives, we were aware that schools were trying to get parental engagement right. But our experience of being engaged as parents was very inconsistent and at times downright terrible! We are both professional communicators, with nearly 50 years of experience between us. We have worked for corporate organisations, in roles with a strong focus on audience engagement, and with individuals wanting to develop their communication skills. We believed that we could use our professional experience and knowledge to make a difference to education through communication, not just for our own children but for all those who follow.

Initially, we didn't quite know how to support our children's education or school-related development. However, we were very supportive of the school leaders and teachers who were clearly trying to do their best to reach out to parents wherever they could, especially on top of so many other priorities. We considered that it might be helpful if we developed some simple approaches to address what we saw as some of the challenges faced by school leaders — in particular, parental engagement.

Our initial action was to listen — the first step in our communication philosophy that you will become familiar with as you read this book. Our intention was to validate our own views and experiences with other parents and school leaders. We are very grateful to the hundreds of parents who have shared their opinions with us and who let us know that we weren't alone in our experiences. Many expressed similar concerns about communication.

Free-form comments from parents, gathered through our research, highlighted the huge level of inconsistency in parental engagement across the UK. Positive comments such as: 'It's a relationship of mutual respect where they listen to and consider the needs of parents in supporting their child's learning,' and 'I feel lucky that my daughter goes to a school which has a lovely happy vibe, that is open to ideas and wants goods links with parents and the community,' were contrasted with negative comments such as: 'They aren't very interested in my viewpoint. I feel they believe they know best,' and 'There is no consistency across the teachers. Lack of communication and preparation for understanding pupils and their needs.'

We knew we had to turn our attention to understanding the situation from a school's perspective too. Once again, we are extremely grateful to the school leaders and teachers who took the time to speak to us at the beginning of our journey. They helped us to understand life from the inside and the scale of challenges that parents just do not see. They told us: 'Building relationships with parents requires time and skill. It's an investment,' and 'Communication is key and needs to be done early on. Over-communicate. Have an open door. Listen.' But once again, there were many negative comments such as: 'Relationships between staff and parents are inconsistent across the school. Expectations are not set or consistently monitored by the SLT,' and 'I think the school could do much more to involve parents in co-planning, development, production and evaluating rather than just telling them what is happening or collecting tokenistic feedback.' But it is possibly this final comment that captured the prevailing mood and the challenge we are seeking to address with this book and our parental engagement model: 'I have been teaching for 20 years and I have seen little difference [in parental engagement] in this time.'

After our initial research, we developed and started to share our simple school communication models. Some of these were published in our first book, *How to Build Communication Success in Your School: A Guide for School Leaders* (Dempster and Robbins, 2017), which received very positive feedback. As we began to work directly with more schools and multi-academy trusts across the country, and with the Department for Education, it became clear to us there was more to be done on parental engagement.

Despite the fact that parental engagement has a proven positive impact on pupil performance, support for teachers is still limited in this area. There are programmes such as the Teacher Classroom Management Program by Incredible Years, based in the United States, which offers assistance to teachers to help parents become more involved in their child's education and promote consistency between home and school.[1] There are organisations like Parentkind in the UK which provide guidance, frameworks, toolkits and resources for schools and teachers,[2] and the Leading Parent Partnership Award which helps schools to work in association with parents and carers to support improved outcomes in all aspects of school life.[3]

---

1   See https://www.incredibleyears.com/programs/teacher/classroom-mgt-curriculum.
2   See https://www.parentkind.org.uk/For-Parents/Parent-Hub/Get-involved-at-school.
3   See https://www.awardplace.co.uk/award/lppa.

Schools are faced with the opposing challenges of parents who won't engage and those who are extremely critical. There are also those who have high expectations of schools and those who are difficult to deal with, often because their high expectations are not being met. Some parents would like to engage more, but the pressures of work, finances, family life and other factors may make this difficult. It is clearly important that schools are supportive of individual situations, working alongside parents and not adding more demands.

People are also bombarded by a huge amount of information every day from computers and phones, including emails, texts, real-time news and social media feeds. All of these are competing for the attention — and precious time — of busy parents that schools are working hard to actively engage in their children's education. Simultaneously, parents' expectations of the education system are changing: they want schools to ensure that their children are prepared for their future careers, with the right mindsets and skills. Other expectations may originate from the backgrounds, values, mindsets and culture of parents in the local community.

Getting parental engagement right will enhance a school's reputation. It will lead to a positive, supportive and happy workplace for the whole school team. And it will help to improve pupils' learning, attendance, behaviour and, the ultimate focus: results. Based on evidence that we will explore, we believe that parental engagement is the missing element in creating a seamless relationship between home and school.

This book is a culmination of our journey so far, and our attempt to fill the gap that currently exists in this critical area — one that has become even more critical in 2021. In fact, right now is a particularly relevant time to pause and take a closer look at parental engagement. We are entering a post-COVID world that has accelerated the change we were already experiencing as part of the fourth industrial revolution (Schwab, 2016). Technology is blurring the lines between the physical, digital and biological. We are seeing the emergence of disruptive technologies and trends such as the internet of things, virtual reality, augmented reality, robotics and artificial intelligence.

These technologies are changing and will continue to change our lives, both at work and at home. During the COVID-19 pandemic, for example, online learning became pretty much the only solution for schools and universities. This experience has opened educators' minds to fresh possibilities for blended learning and new ways of sharing information and communicating with parents. The habits and understanding created during this period have (hopefully) impacted on parents' willingness to provide a positive learning environment at home. It may also have improved the relationship between parents and school because parents have a new-found appreciation for what schools do every day.

Parents' expectations and technological capabilities have also evolved. They are more confident in their ability to use online systems and portals, and so expect schools to provide information in these more flexible and convenient ways.

Increasingly, some parents are starting to doubt the tenets of a traditional education system. This view is supported by work from the World Economic Forum which suggests that we will need different skills and jobs in the future. Their 2018 report, *Towards a Reskilling Revolution*, states that analytical thinking, innovation, active learning, learning strategies, technology design, programming and human skills will continue to rise in prominence. Human skills include creativity, originality, initiative, critical thinking, persuasion, negotiation, attention to detail, resilience, flexibility and complex problem-solving. We will also see an increase in demand for emotional intelligence, leadership, social influence and service orientation.

Most parents want schools to teach their children the skills and mindsets they will need in the future. Yet, many schools are still delivering a curriculum model from the 1960s, where parental engagement was rarely a requirement. Furthermore, education leaders are constantly firefighting and balancing numerous priorities, often unable to focus on the bigger picture, let alone the future. This inertia, combined with increased parental demands, seems destined to create greater friction in school–parent relationships. When parents experience outdated thinking and approaches, trust is lost and frustration kicks in, which then starts to seep into daily relationships and interactions. It may show itself in unexpected ways and can slowly damage a school's ability to work well with parents.

This trust is put on further rocky ground when parents start to question previously respected and reliable sources of information: we are all now far less likely to believe everything we see and read. This has been driven by social media and the fear of fake news. Add in the tensions of identity politics — whether that is gender, age, nationality, ethnicity, sexual orientation, health, physical or mental ability — and the potential to get inclusive parental engagement wrong snowballs.

In developing this book, we carried out quantitative (survey based) and qualitative (interview based) research with parents, school teams and pupils from across the UK to understand the current view of parental engagement in schools. This work was built on existing published research.

We asked parents to define what their child's success at school looked like to them. The top response was for them to be 'happy' (accounting for 29% of all responses), followed by academic success (24%). Next were life skills, including being 'confident' (11%), 'engaged in learning' (10%), 'socialised' (9%) and the 'best they can be' (9%). Interestingly, parents claimed that their child's happiness was more important than pure academic success. This is an important consideration because being happy covers many areas that are relevant to active parental engagement, which is a key area of tension when we consider the importance of school performance tables. Being 'well socialised', which included areas such as having a strong friendship group and good communication skills, also came through strongly.

In our research, pupils reported a strong desire to have the support of their parents, regardless of age bracket: 82% of them told us that their parents' support affected how well they did at school. It confirmed the need for both the push and pull of active parental engagement — a push from the school and a pull from the pupils.

The four pillars of parental engagement model is aimed at anyone in schools who is responsible for parental engagement, whether that is a head teacher, business manager, the school office team or head of communications or marketing. This book will guide you through the following:

- Understanding what good parental engagement is, based on research and the four pillars of our parental engagement model.

- Identifying how you are doing now, so you can understand where there are gaps and therefore how to define your parental engagement plan.

- Developing activities to close the gaps and achieve your plan, supported by templates and an online toolkit.

- Tracking progress against your plan.

There is much more to be done by all stakeholders, including school leaders, educators, policymakers, thought leaders and government, particularly in our uncertain post-pandemic world where we are likely to see an escalation in virtual over human interaction. Our simple parental engagement model is timeless and acknowledges the advantages and benefits of the digital world. We hope that it helps schools to work in partnership with parents, putting children at the heart of everything. We hope that it helps you and your school to make a positive difference to education.

Acknowledgements

This book would not have been possible without the fantastic support from:

Mark Anderson, ICT Evangelist

Claudia Barwell

Neil Dawson, executive principal, Specialist Education Services

Lucy Evans, Frog Education

Ian Gilbert, Independent Thinking

Sharon Gray, NLE, OBE

Daniel Harvey, strategic director for learning and communication, John Henry Newman Catholic College

Lord Jim Knight

Anthony Martin, Exeter College

Dave McPartlin, head teacher, Flakefleet Primary School

Julie Rees, head teacher, Ledbury Primary School

Paul Rose, YouTeachMe

Jenny Ross

Abi Steady, deputy head teacher and specialist leader of education, Ashmount School

Chris Wheeler, principal, Monkton Combe School

All the parents and school team members who took part in our research.

And, of course, our families.

Note from the Authors

Throughout this book we refer to 'parents'. By this we mean anyone who has a responsibility to look after school-aged children and therefore includes single parents, grandparents, extended family, carers, foster parents and legal guardians.

Information, templates and guides to support this book are available at https://fit2communicate.com/fourpillarsbook.

Contents

Introduction

In this book, we aim to get you to the point where you can have a positive conversation with parents. We want you to create the spark for a common focus with parents at your school and their children. We want you to have a clear plan for achieving long-term and sustainable results, and a shared passion to ensure that pupils can be the very best versions of themselves when they leave your school.

But what does the term 'parental engagement' mean? Let us take the easy part first — parental. It simply means relating to a parent or characteristic of a parent. This might be a biological parent or a parental figure, such as a foster parent, family member or other carer. We use 'parental' in the broadest sense in this book to recognise parental figures in their many shapes and forms.

Engagement is a little more ambiguous in its definition. It is often misunderstood, which doesn't help with our ability to achieve this goal. Engagement can be confused with 'persuading' people, for example, to participate. Parental engagement is about more than parents showing up at a parents' evening; simply showing up isn't quite enough. We need parents to be 'actively engaged' throughout their child's time at school, in the secondary phase as well as primary, which requires us to take things to another level. We believe the best way to explain active engagement is to literally visualise what it looks like in practice.

Imagine you are holding a parents' evening at the start of a new school year. You have decided to host an online session now that your school and parents are more comfortable with this form of communication. You are slightly nervous about this as you prefer standing in front of a live audience and seeing the whites of their eyes, but you persist. To your delight, you get a great acceptance level of 96% of parents to your email invitation — far higher than ever before.

The evening arrives and nearly everyone who has accepted is online, ready to listen to you and your team. You are raring to go; as you see it, you already have a group of engaged parents ready to get involved in their children's education. You deliver the session, telling parents about your plans for the year and sharing with them some simple examples of actions they could take to instil good learning habits in their children — for example, you mention some questions they could ask and share a few pictures of positive learning environments. Afterwards, you discuss with your colleagues how well they think the session went. 'Great, sir' and 'You did a good job,

Mrs Richards' are the responses. However, as the year progresses, you hear reports of pupils struggling and Progress 8 scores are below those of previous years. How can this be when you did such a good job of engaging parents early in the first term?

As you are now discovering, being motivated enough to turn up to a parents' evening, whether through a sense of duty or fear, doesn't mean parents are going to be actively engaged. They went away and did not take any of the actions you suggested. Active engagement happens when you find common ground, and this usually starts with listening. How well did you listen to the parents during your virtual parents' evening? Did you ask them beforehand what they wanted to find out about? Or what sort of support they required from you to enable them to better support their own children?

One way to create common ground would be to invite them to the event by email, just like you actually did. However, in addition, you could include an opportunity for them to respond by asking them to state their top, or even top three, challenges regarding supporting their children during the coming year, or their main concerns about their children achieving their goals and being successful. You could ask them to respond directly to you or a colleague by email, or include a link to a simple online survey using a free tool such as Google Forms, or, if you have access to them, a paid platform such as Microsoft Forms, Survey Monkey or via your parent portal. In this way, you can also track their responses, allowing you to follow up with those parents who didn't share their challenges or concerns, thereby really demonstrating your intention to listen to their views.

In preparation for the event, you could review the parent feedback, group it under common headings such as 'time', 'knowledge', 'resistance' and so on, and pick out the key areas. Usually three will suffice, although you may wish to go further if time at the event allows. It is important that you share your analysis of the results with parents, so they all feel they have been heard, even if their concerns did not make the top three that you address. You could then offer some specific practical solutions for each of the main challenges or concerns. You could also consider asking if any parents would like to form a working group to help each other address any of the areas, which is a great way to get them involved and, ultimately, engaged. Finally, be sure to follow up afterwards with some simple and succinct notes or even a personal video.

The impact of active parental engagement on academic outcomes

Despite decades of research confirming that involving families and the community positively contributes to children's academic success, it is still one of the main challenges that many schools, and in particular secondary schools, mention every time they are asked about what difficulties they are facing. According to research conducted with 10,000 students in the United States, parenting is more important than schools in improving academic achievement (Dufur et al., 2013). The researchers compared measures of 'family social capital' and 'school social capital'. Pupils with two involved parents enjoyed school 51% more and achieved higher grades more often than those who didn't have involved parents.

Family social capital included areas such as whether parents checked homework, attended school meetings and events, how much trust they gave their child and how often pupils reported discussing school activities with their parents. School social capital measured a school's ability to serve as a positive environment for learning, and included areas such as pupil participation in extracurricular activities, if the school contacted parents, teacher morale, conflict in school, if teachers responded to individual pupil needs, and an overall measure of the school environment that covered attendance and discipline. It was found that even in schools with low social capital, pupils were more likely to excel if their family social capital scores were high.

Toby Parcel, professor of sociology at North Carolina State University and a co-author of the study, said: 'In part what's going on is that, when the children's parents are engaged in those ways, then the children pick up on it. They think, "School is important. My parents think it's important," and that increases their attachment to education, which translates into better achievement' (Molnar, 2012).

While this is not the only study into the impact of parental engagement on pupil outcomes, it used a significantly large sample and covered a wide range of social circumstances. John Hattie found that 'the effect of parental engagement over a student's school career is equivalent to adding two or three years to that student's education' (quoted in NASBM, 2016: 4). After surveying more than 3,170 pupils and 200 teachers, researchers found that children are more likely to succeed if teachers have positive perceptions of parents (University of Missouri, 2017). This study is interesting as it suggests there is a 'Pygmalion' and 'Golem' effect (Friedrich et al., 2015). The Pygmalion effect refers to the positive influence that expectations can have on others' performance; the Golem effect has the opposite result, as it reduces self-esteem and performance.

Implications for parental engagement are significant. Having engaged parents from the start, teachers are subconsciously more likely to have confidence in the child and therefore encourage them. Conversely, if the same teacher perceives a child's parents to be disengaged in their education, they are subconsciously likely to project less confidence in that child.

According to Professor Keith Herman of University of Missouri College of Education, 'these findings show the importance of teacher–parent connections and also the need for training teachers on how to create effective relationships with all parents' (University of Missouri, 2017). We believe that it is the second part of Herman's statement that presents the biggest challenge for many secondary schools, because it is an area they simply don't address with any intent. Communicating between school and home is simple compared to the complexity of building trusted relationships. Training is not offered consistently to all potential teachers in the UK, despite the compelling evidence of positive outcomes, which go far beyond happy parents and happy pupils.

A report by the Department for Education and Skills on the impact of parental support on pupil achievement (Desforges and Abouchaa, 2003) concluded that the extent and form of parental involvement is strongly influenced by social class, maternal level of education, maternal psycho-social health, material deprivation, single parent status and, to a lesser degree, family ethnicity. This is important as we believe that active parental engagement does not discriminate. It requires an approach that is inclusive of all parents. The lifestyle choices, career aspirations, self-awareness, ability to adapt to change and community involvement of pupils should not be limited by social class, education, deprivation, mental health, parental status or ethnicity.

A World Economic Forum white paper titled *Resetting the Future of Work Agenda: Disruption and Renewal in a Post-COVID World* (2020) calls for lifelong learning cultures. This aligns strongly with our own research into what parents want, which is more frequent communication and interactions, guided by the parental engagement model.

A pupil perspective

Pupils need a network of people around them, working closely to ensure they are supported in their learning and development, and guided through the ups and downs of growing up. This network should include parents and schools which work in the best interests of the child, communicating regularly so everyone understands the child's needs, interests and concerns in the context of the home environment. This communication should begin when a child starts school, not just when things go wrong.

Many young people are feeling increasingly overwhelmed by our rapidly changing world, which is negatively impacting on their mental health and well-being. Anxiety, depression, self-harm and suicide regularly appear in news headlines, and bullying (whether in person or online) is all too common. Social deprivation leaves some children too hungry to learn, potentially pushing them into undesirable ways of life just to survive their peers' and life's pressures. According to a survey from the Royal College of Psychiatrists, young people are also suffering from eco-anxiety — feelings of helplessness, guilt, panic and anger about the fate of the planet (Cuff, 2020).

An Action for Children and YouGov survey in 2019 involving both children and adults revealed that children, parents and grandparents fear that childhood is getting worse. All three generations agreed that bullying (online and offline) was the biggest problem preventing a good childhood. In addition, there was an increased pressure to 'fit in'. Children are worried about poverty and homelessness, closely followed by terrorism. Some children have to take on caring responsibilities for siblings and even parents, who may have mental or physical health issues. With people living longer, they may also have to help with the care of a grandparent.

At the same time, there has been a collapse in investment from the UK government into children's services. The impact on our children is a ticking time bomb and one that schools cannot solve alone. Without the support of parents and the broader community — and, of course, increased funding — the outlook is challenging.

In 2018, the BBC reported that the number of children being home-educated between 2014 and 2017 in the UK had increased by 40% (Issimdar, 2018). This trend has continued, and is likely to do so even after the COVID-19 pandemic has settled, mainly due to mental ill health or other factors, including keeping children at home to avoid potential exclusion due to disruptive classroom behaviour. Parents of children with special educational needs (SEN), in particular, do not feel that they are being supported adequately and are being treated by schools as a problem. This was reiterated in Ofsted's 2017/18 annual report, which expressed concerns that pupils receiving SEN support were five times more likely to be permanently excluded (Ofsted, 2018). Clearly, a strong school–parent relationship always makes a positive difference, but even more so for pupils facing difficult circumstances.

Case study: Building strong school–home relationships at Ashmount

Ashmount is a special school based in Loughborough for pupils between the ages of 4 and 19. The school team support children with a range of special educational needs, who come from a wide area and are often transported to school in local authority vehicles. As a result, communication with parents is often limited.

What was the challenge or opportunity?

The school was aware that parents didn't have much time to read long reports or write in home–school diaries. They were simply very busy — attending medical appointments and physiotherapy sessions, picking up other children, sorting out housing problems and so much more, as well as dealing with the avalanche of associated paperwork. And things often don't go to plan at home, particularly with children with additional needs, so even the best laid parental engagement plans didn't always work.

The school already had some parental engagement activities, including annual reviews, parents' evenings, an open-door policy and open afternoons where parents and children learned together, covering topics such as healthy cooking and breakfasts. The uptake was often limited to a few parents who attended events regularly. They tended to be those who lived close to school and maybe didn't work.

Abi Steady, deputy head teacher and specialist leader of education at Ashmount, and her team knew they needed to do more, but they didn't want to put pressure on parents when they were already emotionally and physically overwhelmed. They wanted to be sensitive to everything going on around the families, but also to create more opportunities to bring parents closer to the school and for parents to be able to enjoy learning at home with their children.

Homework was another challenge. Abi said: 'Only a few families were engaging with homework and many parents opted out of homework altogether because they felt it would put too much pressure on them and their child.' A few parents also reported that supporting their child at home was tough due to the complexity of the child's learning needs and sometimes their own difficulties. Having tried lots of different ways of setting homework — whether it was creative, maths or English — or changing the frequency, nothing really seemed to help.

What actions did the Ashmount team take?

Through a chance encounter, Abi came across YouTeachMe (www.youteachmetoo. com), an online service that enables schools to use video to improve learning and teaching. Abi could see significant benefits in using video to support parents, as it is easier to engage with than book-based materials, and also how the service could support many children, regardless of their personal needs.

YouTeachMe helped the school to provide personalised video messages for children to listen to at home with their parents to support homework tasks. Parents can access a personalised library of videos, differentiated for their individual child. To access the videos, they simply scan a QR code or use a web link. The school makes adding a username and password very simple.

About the results

Abi said: 'Parents seeing what and how their child is being taught in school has given them the confidence to get involved with extra activities at home. For example, parents are taking their children to the library to build on the learning happening at school.'

The school previously shared Makaton signs (based on gestures used in British Sign Language) and safety information during lessons with all pupils. These can now be shared before the lesson takes place via video, so the time within sessions is used much more effectively.

YouTeachMe enabled the staff at Ashmount to safely deliver both teaching and support materials into homes during the COVID-19 lockdowns. The children have really enjoyed the wide-ranging videos sent to assist and inspire their learning. They especially loved seeing Abi in her kitchen wearing her martial arts uniform! Parents, learners and staff are enthused by the YouTeachMe video approach and have engaged with it fully.

The main challenge is the digital divide, so the school has been careful not to put pressure on those children or parents with limited access to the internet. They know which families have the required technology and ensure that those who can't access the internet do an 'in school' YouTeachMe session before the related lesson.

Ashmount also uses Tapestry (https://tapestry.info), a secure online learning journal that helps staff and families to celebrate their children's learning and development. It also allows the school to post videos/photos online and parents to post back. Both parents and the school can also comment, so the conversation continues. The school team take the time to positively reinforce the great work the parents are doing, and this is well received.

A parental perspective

Parents who are fearful about the state of the world are putting ever more pressure on their children and on schools. This includes passing exams with the highest grades and going to the 'right' schools and colleges, so their children can be 'winners' in today's increasingly competitive society. They see education as a passport to success, but it can come at a high cost to children's mental health and social development.

This, in turn, is reflected in the pressure applied to teachers and schools in general. However, we are also seeing a shift in job recruitment on the emphasis on exam results. Recruiters are finding that more organisations are placing a greater focus on experience over exam results (Aspire, 2019). This trend seems set to continue, with a stronger reliance on technology to analyse the suitability and potential of candidates.

Many parents in England view Ofsted reports as a critical way to understand how suitable a school will be for their child. Ofsted clearly values the views of parents, so the parent survey is an important element of the Ofsted inspection. They have also reinforced the crucial role that parents play in supporting schools with their child's learning – for example, Ofsted state that schools should not be expected to 'do parents' jobs' for them (Ofsted, 2018: 20). They also add the 'startling fact that 70% of staff surveyed by the Association of Teachers and Lecturers (ATL) reported more children arriving in Reception unable to use a toilet compared with 2011' (Ofsted, 2018: 19). These remarks received a mixed reaction. A partnership approach to building a positive relationship between schools, parents and their children is necessary – one that does not point blame at any particular party.

There are also parents who believe that their children need more than just good grades to be successful in life, as was illustrated in our own research with parents: 29% of them told us that success at school was their child being 'happy' (ahead of academic success at 24%). Their demands are much more focused on supporting their child as an individual. Schools that embrace this philosophy tend to have innovative or progressive approaches to education that equip each child with the life skills they need to be resilient, balanced and able to give back positively to the world.

Schools also need to consider the changing shape of families in the UK. The 2019 Modern Families report stated that of the 14 million dependent children living in families, 64% live in a married couple family. The percentage of dependent children living in cohabiting families increased from 7% to 15% between 1996 and 2018, but the percentage living in single parent families changed little. Dual earner households are normal in the UK and situations with both parents working full-time increased from 26% to 31% between 2001 and 2013. The employment rate for mothers was 74% in 2018 – an increase of 5.1% over the previous five years (Bright Horizons and Working Families, 2019: 4). The shifts in family structures require schools to carefully consider how they reach parents and the demands they put on them during normal working hours (although some parents will be working shifts outside of those hours).

Parents are under pressure from work, financial and family demands which have been intensified by the COVID-19 pandemic. The Modern Families report states that 29% of parents describe their work–life well-being as poor often or all the time, and 38% said it was poor some of the time (Bright Horizons and Working Families, 2019: 17). If parents' well-being is not being fully supported at work, this increases the risk of mental and physical health issues and makes supporting their child's learning and development even more challenging.

The changing cultural make-up of the UK brings challenges and opportunities for parental engagement. Culture, as well as intimate social relationships, influences parenting styles and shape a child's personality (UKEssays, 2018). In 2011, the total population of England and Wales was 56.1 million and 86% of the population was white. People from Asian ethnic groups made up the second largest population percentage (7.5%), followed by black ethnic groups (3.3%), mixed/multiple ethnic groups (2.2%) and other ethnic groups (1.0%).[1] This is only the broader picture; the influence of different cultures will be stronger in certain areas of the country where there are larger ethnic communities. Schools need to understand their local neighbourhoods and build approaches that enable them to engage with changing demographics and diverse perspectives in an inclusive way.

---

1   See https://www.ons.gov.uk/census/2011census/2011censusdata.

A teacher perspective

The third cornerstone in the school–home relationship is teachers. Teacher recruitment and retention is a huge pinch point. Although the National Foundation for Educational Research reported in 2017 that more teachers are now joining the profession than leaving, there is concern that the number of teachers isn't growing quickly enough to meet the projected rise in pupil numbers, particularly in secondary schools (Lynch and Worth, 2017).

Having teachers in jobs is one thing, but ensuring that they are fit and able to teach to a high standard is another. Professor Jonathan Glazzard and Dr Anthea Rose, from the Carnegie School of Education at Leeds Beckett University, looked at the impact of teacher well-being and mental health on pupil progress in primary schools. Most teachers agreed that a teacher's well-being affects their performance as an education professional, especially their ability to teach in the classroom. 'Teachers reported a number of work-related stress triggers including busy times of the year, such as assessment periods; the pressure of extra curricula activities; the unexpected; keeping up with the pace of change; and changes in school leadership' (Glazzard and Rose, 2019: 4).

To support great teaching and a teacher's ability to engage with parents, we need to equip them with the capabilities, confidence and time to do this effectively — without adding even more pressure. In our research, school team members told us that the most effective way of communicating with parents were parents' evenings (32%), followed by opportunities for parents to meet teachers or tutors (19%) and pupil performances for parents (17%). Other activities that were considered helpful in engaging parents were parent workshops, evenings on the curriculum and revision, parent/pupil activities on specific days, parent cafes, stay and read sessions, celebrations of learning events, home visits and Family Links parent groups.

School team members told us that they would appreciate having clearer instructions to share with parents, better materials and technology, training in how to effectively engage parents and leadership support, particularly during difficult conversations with parents (the most challenging scenarios concerned engaging with highly critical parents and parents who are simply difficult to deal with). Developing active engagement with parents is not a skill that is currently part of teacher training.

We have already observed how important active parental engagement is in ensuring positive outcomes for pupils. We provide some guidance for teachers in this book, but we hope to see skills to support creating active engagement becoming standard in teacher training in the UK and beyond in a very short time. This would include how to identify and apply communication preferences, both their own and those of others. Given that our ability to communicate contributes up to 85% of our success (Mann, 1918: 106–107), it is difficult to understand why this is not already a fundamental part of teacher education.

Time for a rethink

There are many factors to consider when defining what active parental engagement should look like in our changing world. Ultimately, actively engaging with someone is about a relationship. However, we believe that active parental engagement is more than just what happens between school and parents: it is a three-way relationship between school, parents and pupils — with pupils firmly at the centre.

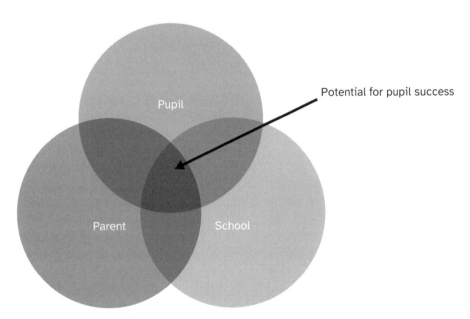

Involving pupils in the parental engagement challenge seems an obvious approach to us as they are the common motivator for schools and parents. Young people today are incredibly well informed: knowledge is at their fingertips and friends are at the end of a phone. It is normal for them to communicate constantly with their peers every day. However, when it comes to giving them the opportunity to share how best to communicate with their own parents, they are mute. Simply left out of the loop.

Potentially, pupils are better placed than schools to communicate with parents. While a school is often forced to take a mass communication approach with parents, pupils can communicate with them in a wholly individual way — when they have the right support and cues from school and parents. In our research, pupils told us they want their parents to do all of the following:

- Ask them about how things are going at school.
- Give them the space and quiet to do schoolwork.
- Sit with them and help them.
- Attend school events so they know what is going on.
- Take them to places to extend their learning.
- Ensure they have the equipment they need in order to learn.

These activities are very specific to each pupil. Some are very basic and obvious; it is often what is taken for granted that is most easily missed. Not asking a child how their day went may not, in itself, have a significant or long-lasting impact on their learning. However, when paired with a child not having space or equipment, there is suddenly a significant disconnect. Imagine a child's inner voice saying: 'If my parent never asks me how I'm doing at school and won't allow me the time and space to study, school can't really be that important, can it?'

We are not suggesting that schools should stop communicating directly with parents and leave it to their children. Our own research with pupils tells us that, despite what they may say to their friends, parents of secondary school pupils continue to have a huge impact on their lives. The opportunity for schools to create active parental engagement comes from recognising the important and active role that pupils can play in the process. Clearly, there needs to be a level of standardisation, but why can't pupils be trusted and empowered as an equal element in the school–parent–pupil relationship?

Our discussions with pupils from Years 7, 8 and 9 revealed that schools need to help parents understand how to support their children's learning and development — for example, through how-to guides and videos. Pupils talked about creating an environment that was fun and interactive for parents, and shared their thoughts on a culture where schools involve their parents more as partners rather than as customers. They also shared their personal experiences of schools' communication with parents — many of them acting as the go-between for busy parents or parents whose grasp of English wasn't good enough to understand what they were being told by the school.

Between 2010 and 2018, Save the Children UK ran the Families and Schools Together (FAST) programme, which helped to tackle the educational inequality that existed between poorer children and their better-off classmates.[2] FAST built stronger bonds between parents, schools and communities to ensure children got the support they needed to do their best at school. When the first randomised controlled trial of FAST was published (Education Endowment Foundation, 2018), it found that the programme was an effective mechanism for engaging parents in their children's early education.

FAST also had a positive impact on children's social and behavioural outcomes – remarkably, for the whole year group and not just the children who had participated. Some 83% of parents who began FAST attended six or more sessions, which was an unusually high retention rate. This trend was also seen in an earlier study that looked at the merits of FAST compared to a parent communication campaign called Family Education (FAME) – essentially, a series of booklets sent to parents with follow-up mail shots and phone calls. Just 4% of FAME families attended the formal school presentation at the end of the campaign (McDonald et al., 2006: 29).

FAST has evolved into an eight-week programme, now called Families Connect, which helps parents to support their children's learning in three key areas: literacy and language development, numeracy and emotional development. It provides parents and carers with a series of activities, techniques and games they can do with their children at home. Each activity encourages parents and children to spend quality time together by talking about specific topics and reflecting on what they already do to support their children's learning. Parents are also invited to informal workshops to discuss the science behind the programme's activities.

There are great lessons to be learned from FAST and Families Connect. They are short-term programmes for targeted children. However, current technology such as personal mobile devices allows for more forward-thinking and ongoing collaboration with regard to providing an individual experience for each family. We believe a longer-term parental engagement model goes beyond simply sharing information and includes the principle of involving pupils and parents working together. For example, a situation where schools use simple mobile technology to share information between pupils and their parents could create an inclusive 'family learning' opportunity.

---

2   See https://www.savethechildren.org.uk/what-we-do/uk-work/in-schools/fast.

Schools have tried many approaches to bridge the gap between home and school. An Education Endowment Foundation review of the evidence on parental engagement across 150 schools found they were using more than 35 different parental engagement interventions (van Poortvliet et al., 2019). We believe that schools need to be supported to develop a new mindset and planned approaches to building strong and long-lasting parent relationships that will benefit pupils. It is a mindset that involves putting the child at the centre of everything, as well as schools putting themselves in the shoes of parents rather than trying to tell parents what to do.

For such a critical and heavily researched area, there is very little guidance readily available with practical steps for schools to put in place easily. As a result, we have developed a parental engagement model based on the four pillars of knowledge, environment, culture and communication.

A parental engagement model for the 21st century

We believe that parents need to have the *knowledge* that their involvement is fundamental and know how to get involved.

Schools need to create an *environment* that supports active parental engagement — at home, in school and online.

There need to be a *culture* whereby school team members act consistently in the eyes of parents, there is a relationship based on mutual trust and each parent feels they are getting personal support, even if it is through a wider medium.

Finally, *communication* needs to be simple to understand, non-threatening, fully inclusive and must recognise the efforts of parents.

In summary, the four pillars of parental engagement are based on the changing needs of parents and pupils. They support schools to consider and strengthen parents' knowledge about their critical role, create a safe and welcoming school environment supported through a home environment and habits that promote learning, and foster a school culture that builds trusted relationships with parents and communication that recognises basic human needs — to be listened to, to be valued and to be simply informed or involved.

The four pillars model is not dependent on a certain level of finance being available to a school, specific demographics or even academic performance. It is accessible and inclusive for all schools. However, it requires strong leadership from the outset to ensure that the school stays the course and doesn't get blown off track when faced with short-term targets or pressing financial challenges. It is often easier for school leaders to choose what might appear to be the easier option with parents and maintain the status quo, leaving the four pillars model for another year. But the opportunity cost of doing so can be huge and devastating, especially when it may require just a simple family-based intervention to create long-term behaviour changes (Education Endowment Foundation, 2018).

There are common challenges for parents, and therefore schools, across the UK. For example, if a parent has had a poor personal experience of education then they may bring this negativity with them — perhaps not wanting to speak with teachers or even go into school. In this case, a parent is starting from a point of disengagement and potentially needs more support in the early days. Our own research has highlighted this as an important area for consideration: 72% of parents said they had a positive experience of school, 12% had a neutral experience and 16% had a negative experience. While the proportion of parents stating that they had a negative experience at school was lower than we had anticipated, it is still an issue that head teachers may want to address (Graham, 2017), particularly as parents who did have a bad experience were less likely to complete our research survey.

We asked parents which single word they would use to describe how they felt when they went into their child's school. Some 74% of parents used positive words, which is fantastic; however, just over a quarter of the words that they used to describe how they felt were negative. The learning we have incorporated into this book comes from both the positive and negative responses. The top five positive and negative words that parents used were:

	Positive	Negative
1.	Welcome	Anxious
2.	Proud	Intimidated
3.	Lucky	Apprehensive
4.	Happy	Worried
5.	Fine	Indifferent

There are many simple things that schools can do to support the positive emotions parents feel when they visit their child's school and diminish the negative ones.

Four pillars of parental engagement

A step-by-step framework for schools to ensure pupils can be at their best.

Knowledge

- ✔ Parents, school team and pupils **know what is expected** of them in the partnership.

- ✔ Parents know **why, when and how to support** their children's learning.

- ✔ Parents are **able to use school technology**, including portals, apps and tools.

- ✔ Parents know how to access and understand their **children's progress information**.

- ✔ Parents know **whom to contact for help** and when they can expect a response.

Environment

- ✔ The school team create a school **environment that welcomes** and supports parents.

- ✔ Parents understand what a **home environment** that supports learning looks like and are supported in creating this.

- ✔ The school creates an **online environment** where parents find what they need easily.

- ✔ Parents are encouraged to share their school experiences to **support continuous improvement and learning**.

- ✔ The school and parents **respect time** commitments.

Culture

✔ School leaders build a **planned school culture** that supports parents, pupils and the school.

✔ The school supports the building of **trusted relationships** between the school team, parents and pupils.

✔ The school team understands and **respects parents' beliefs**, culture, expectations and parenting style.

✔ The school supports **parental involvement** in initiatives and bodies.

✔ The school **involves pupils and parents together**.

Communication

✔ Parents receive **simple and easy-to-access information** that is clear and consistent.

✔ The school is focused on listening to **parents and pupils**.

✔ School team members are appropriately **trained in communicating confidently** with parents.

✔ The school supports parents to **communicate with their children**.

✔ Parents are **recognised and feel valued** for their great work.

Acknowledging that some individuals had a bad experience of school can help teachers to be more understanding and avoid adopting a one-size-fits-all approach to parental communication.

Another issue is school communications. In most schools we have worked with, these are normally uncoordinated across the school — nobody knows what else is being sent to parents at the same time. These are generally anonymous bulk messages and are often irrelevant to many parents. It has been shown that emails with personalised subject lines generate 50% higher open rates (Mohsin, 2020). A parent may receive five such non-personal bulk emails within the space of a few hours from their child's school (often on a Friday afternoon). They are unlikely to read the first of them, let alone all of them.

In the following chapters, we will explore the four pillars of parental engagement and share examples of what we consider to be best practice and innovative thinking, along with some common pitfalls to avoid.

Chapter 1

The Four Pillars of Parental Engagement Model

Whether or not you are aware that you have made one, every school makes a promise to its parents. This is created through what you and other people have said (and implied) about your school. Parents have formed expectations that need to be fulfilled. Your promise needs to be kept; otherwise, you risk giving parents a negative perception, perhaps even a negative experience, of your school. This will lead to difficult conversations with parents about the school falling short, followed by lots of negativity and potentially damaging feedback – possibly parents moving their child to another school.

Greater parental choice has led to more competition among schools and, in turn, a greater focus on pupil attraction and retention. To excel, schools need to adopt a customer experience mindset to parental engagement. The parent experience should be intentional and planned, carefully guiding parents through the critical moments of truth, when your school demonstrates how it will deliver on its promise to the school team, pupils, local community and, of course, parents.

The parent experience begins before their child goes to your school. Parents start to form an impression of what you are promising through what your marketing materials (e.g. your website) say about life at your school, what other parents say about your school and how your school and pupils are perceived in the local community. Every touchpoint plays a part in parental experience.

When you actively manage this experience through parental engagement, parents will have a positive impression of your school, which looks like the figure on page 20.

If you can deliver the parent promise (almost) all of the time, you will build trust and strong parental relationships that will support you in the good and the more difficult times. As an additional benefit, parents will talk positively about your school as advocates.

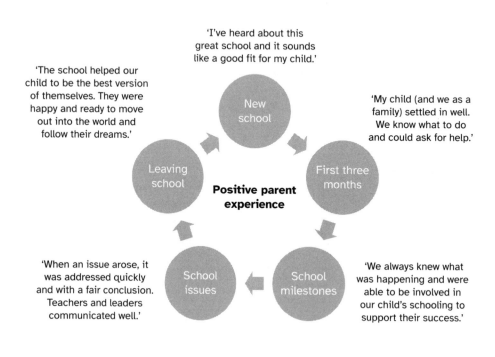

'I've heard about this great school and it sounds like a good fit for my child.'

'My child (and we as a family) settled in well. We know what to do and could ask for help.'

'We always knew what was happening and were able to be involved in our child's schooling to support their success.'

'When an issue arose, it was addressed quickly and with a fair conclusion. Teachers and leaders communicated well.'

'The school helped our child to be the best version of themselves. They were happy and ready to move out into the world and follow their dreams.'

New school

First three months

School milestones

School issues

Leaving school

Positive parent experience

The four pillars of active parental engagement

The four pillars model is designed to create a great parent experience at your school. The model contains the four pillars of knowledge, environment, culture and communication. Each pillar has five outcomes. Achieving each of these will deliver active parental engagement for your school.

Keep in mind that each pillar should not be mutually exclusive. Working on one area of the model is likely to have an impact on other areas. For example, when you start to build parents' knowledge about just how much positive influence they can have on their children's learning, this may cause them to demand more information from you, which could have an effect on the communication pillar.

The four pillars parental engagement model is based on our belief that pupils have a significant influence on the engagement level of their parents. It is not simply a one-way process from school to parent, which is the general philosophy to which most parental engagement models seem to adhere. When you have successfully implemented the four pillars model, you will benefit from all of the following:

- You will develop a positive and trusted alliance with parents to support pupils.
- Parents and pupils will have a positive perception of your school.
- Your school will understand what is important to parents.
- Parents and pupils will feel involved and want to participate more in school life.
- An ongoing conversation about learning will spill out into the community.

We will now look at each pillar of the parental engagement model in more detail, so you can identify the outcomes you should be achieving for each one. In further chapters, we will help you to understand how you are doing against each of these pillars and what actions you can take to close any gaps, so that you can achieve your parental engagement goals.

Pillar 1: Knowledge

'Knowledge is power', as the saying goes. No one, not even the smartest of people, is able to take actions based on things they don't know. Parents are no different — so, knowledge is the first pillar of the parental engagement model.

Clear expectations

Outcome: *Parents, school team and pupils know what is expected of them in the partnership.*

The need to set clear expectations is obvious and fundamental, which is why it is first in our list. What this looks like to school team members might be much more apparent than to parents and pupils. For example, it is certain that your school has performance outcomes and expectations for the school team related to their roles, even if these do not focus specifically on parental engagement. The Department for Education's 2019 model teacher appraisal policy is not statutory, but schools can choose to adopt it. The policy states: 'The objectives set for each teacher will, if achieved, contribute to the school's plans for improving the school's educational provision and performance and improving the education of pupils at that school' (Department for Education, 2019: 8). There is no specific mention of parental engagement, although, of course, it is implied throughout. That said, based on our experience of other organisations, it is often said that 'what gets measured gets done'. This may seem like a simple tick, but there is more to it than initially meets the eye. Specific actions such as 'Understand X about each pupil's family by X date' would be a simple and demonstrable way to confirm what is expected of school team members (not just teachers) in their relationship with parents and pupils.

Parents, on the other hand, might be forgiven for having an expectation that it is the school's responsibility to engage them. That is simply not true. The hypnotist Paul McKenna has said that he can't hypnotise someone who doesn't want to be hypnotised, and the same applies to engagement. Now, engagement isn't in any way the same as hypnosis (actually it's much more difficult!), but what it does have in common with it is that people who don't want to be engaged probably won't be. We are sure you can think of parents who you would put into this category. These individuals, along with parents at the other extreme – the eager ones responding to your emails, commenting on your Facebook posts and being the first on the list for parents' evenings – may not be your principal target audience. Excluding these extremes, you are likely to be left with 75–95% of parents in your school, and these are the people you should be targeting. You need to ensure that they know that engagement is also their responsibility. This could be through the school–parent–pupil agreement you set up with them when their children join your school, a specific written communication or even a workshop. Either way, you need to make it crystal clear that there are shared responsibilities on both sides.

Finally, pupils – who are possibly the least likely members of the relationship to expect to have a responsibility for parental engagement. After all, it is all about the pupils, so why would they have any responsibility in the process? This is what we believe sets our model apart from anything that has gone before. Taking a family approach, and explicitly listening to pupils, will reap benefits over the long term. Many schools will have a pupil code of conduct, or something similar, that will tend to focus on pupil *behaviour* rather than pupil *involvement*. We believe that pupils should have explicit responsibilities that set out their role in engaging their parents. This could be part of a pupil code of conduct. However, it should be supported by something more practical and engaging, such as a pupil workshop which explores how pupils think their parents could be more involved.

Why, when and how

Outcome: *Parents know why, when and how to support their children's learning.*

The rationale for the importance of parental engagement, as outlined in the introduction to this book, should be communicated to every single parent at your school, in a way that connects with their motivations and overcomes their concerns.

Our experience is that many school leaders assume that parents understand their critical role in their children's education. The reality is that many parents will support their children, but don't really understand the impact of them being fully engaged, partially engaged or completely disengaged. It is important that your school explains to parents exactly why their active engagement is necessary to the future success of their children, beyond the headlines they can read in the newspapers. This needs to be explained in terms that resonate and connect with what is valued by parents, not just schools. We would recommend using some of the evidence presented in the introduction as a starting point.

To explain the when and how, it would be fantastic to invite parents of recent pupils into your school to share their stories during an event or ask them to record a personal testimony that you could share afterwards. This could be supported by school resources such as a parent guidebook. The impact is likely to be greater coming from parents who are similar to them, and with whom they can identify, than hearing the same stories from a teacher. Obviously, the more diverse your parent champions, the more disposed the broader school audience will be to identify with them.

If this isn't a possibility, you will need to think about specific examples that could apply to your own school situation and communicate these in clear and easy-to-digest ways. Whatever approach you take, it needs to be relevant to the different parent types at your school. We will discuss this in more detail later in the book.

From our research

How do parents feel about supporting their child's learning?

Only 51% of parents felt valued by their child's school for supporting their child's learning; 21% felt undervalued and 28% expressed no preference. This is an important finding that schools could easily act upon. As human beings, we will generally do more of something when we feel valued for doing it. For example, a survey from the American Psychological Association (2012) found that feeling valued at work was linked to better physical and mental health, as well as higher levels of engagement, satisfaction and motivation — all the things that lead to healthy and productive relationships.

Technology

Outcome: *Parents are able to use school technology, including portals, apps and tools.*

In our experience, many schools make new portals, apps or online tools available to parents, but fail to provide adequate support and capability so they know how to use them. In some cases, they are introduced via an email with a link and parents are left to work out the rest for themselves. Best practice involves sharing new apps, websites and portals with the school team first, so they can use and explain them confidently. They are then introduced to the pupils, who are often the ones supporting parents. Finally, parents are given the opportunity to try them out — for example, at a parents' event where they can be supported by members of the school team.

It is easy to assume that your new digital tool is simple to use, but from the perspective of a parent faced with trying to navigate new technology to understand how their child is doing at school or to book an appointment with a teacher, it can be extremely daunting and an immediate barrier to engaging with the school.

It is also essential to bear in mind the difficulties faced by parents who don't have a computer or internet access. Those relying on a mobile phone may find that data caps and small screens prevent them from accessing some online tools. It is important to be sensitive to these situations and support these parents with alternatives where you can.

By understanding how we adapt to new ways of doing things and what makes us want to change — such as being open to using novel apps and online tools — schools can take a simple and effective human-focused approach to introducing new technology for parents. This will ensure that parents use the new tools and resources, and that your school achieves all of the intended benefits, including saving you time and money. The same approach to introducing new technology to parents can be used each year, updating it as required. You can find a simple template to help you to introduce new technology within your school at: https://fit2communicate.com/fourpillarsbook.

Progress

Outcome: *Parents know how to access and understand their children's progress information.*

Knowing how their child is doing at school is fundamental to any parent being sufficiently well informed to support them. 'How was your day?' or 'How did you get on in the latest exam?' will elicit varying levels of response from children, some more open and honest than others! In some schools, it is a once-a-term report card taken home by pupils; in others, the information is available online and regularly updated. This outcome is directly linked to the previous technology one: if information is available online or through an app, you need to ensure that parents can and know how to access it.

We would recommend that you set expectations at the start of every year in terms of when the school will provide parents with formal progress information and where they can find interim updates (if possible). Given that how grades are represented can change over time, it can be pretty confusing as a parent who hasn't been at school for more than 20 years. There is plenty of literature available online for parents who have the time or desire to search it out. However, a really helpful and impactful engagement activity is to ensure that every parent understands the grading system used to determine their child's progress scores.

Contacts

Outcome: *Parents know whom to contact for help and when they can expect a response.*

There is much more to this topic than you might initially imagine. Schools report that certain people's inboxes or school hotlines are overloaded with parent enquiries, and parents report not receiving a timely response from school to their enquiries. There is nothing more disengaging than feeling that your voice is being ignored, or at least not heard quickly enough.

Quite often, the underlying issue is that parents don't know whom to contact when they have a specific query, or whether it should be the same contact point as when they have a general query. There are various factors that will affect what this looks like at your school, not least the number of pupils on roll and the number of staff in the school office. However, it is an issue that can be easily resolved by putting a few simple processes in place and providing clear communication to parents giving specific contact details for specific circumstances. Managing parents' expectations here is key, so saying, 'We will respond to you within 48 hours if you send an email to this address' or 'If your query is urgent, please contact XXX', is better than having them wait in frustration. Managing expectations in this way gives parents an alternative contact option if needed, so they will feel that their voice is important, which will help to boost their levels of engagement with the school.

Pillar 2: Environment

The environment has a major influence on how people feel and behave. It can refer to physical surroundings or to the conditions in which people find themselves. The whole school environment is the second of our four pillars. It plays a critical part in the degree to which parents actively engage with the school. By 'whole school' we mean more than the physical buildings: this will include the school's online presence, parents' and pupils' experience of dealing with school team members and even their own home learning environment.

Welcome and support

Outcome: *The school team create a school environment that welcomes and supports parents.*

The school itself should be welcoming, especially as some parents find schools to be a daunting environment. As we saw in the introduction, when we asked parents what word best describes how they feel when they enter their child's school, many used negative words such as anxious, intimidated, apprehensive, worried and indifferent.

There are various ways to create a positive experience for parents when they visit the school, including the physical environment that can be seen and touched and the non-physical conditions.

When a parent walks into your school, they may see signage, a front desk, your school team, pupils' work on the walls or inspirational quotes. It may be light and bright, or it may be darker due to its age or design. The building may be echoey or loud. Parents may hear the hum of chatter or the laughter of pupils. They will be greeted by certain members of staff who will influence their first impressions of the school based on how welcoming they seem. Your cleaners may use a particular cleaning product that creates a familiar (but maybe not always positive) smell in your school.

Some of these physical factors can be changed at little cost and others to some degree only. Consider how you can make your school into a friendly and hospitable environment, where people are positive and everyone is instantly made to feel welcome.

From our research

How does their child's school make parents feel?

56% of parents said that their child's school does extremely well at making them feel comfortable and welcome when they visit, with 29% saying they do this quite well.

40% of parents said their child's school does extremely well at giving parents opportunities to talk to tutors/teachers, with 37% saying they do this quite well.

39% of parents said their child's school does extremely well at giving parents notice about events and when they need to attend school, with 39% saying they do this quite well.

Home support

Outcome: *Parents understand what a home environment that supports learning looks like and are supported in creating this.*

Learning at home with parents enables children to achieve more. When children talk openly with their parents about their day at school and other things, they will achieve more educationally than those who don't (Daniel, 2015). In addition, when parents read aloud to their children, they achieve better educational outcomes than children whose parents don't (Nicola, 2017).

In our research, 72% of parents said they felt confident in supporting their child's learning at home and 93% believed that their support made a difference to their child's learning at school. However, in focus groups, we often hear from pupils that they simply want a place to learn at home, uninterrupted by others. Chaotic home environments and expectations for children to look after their siblings, including doing work at home with them, can make simple homework assignments very difficult.

Effective home support starts with ensuring that both parents and school are clear about how home and school environments overlap in terms of pupils' learning. This requires that both teachers and parents are on the same page with regard to what they are trying to achieve. Together they can create positive attitudes to learning in each pupil. Children may not immediately see their parents and teachers as having common goals regarding their education, so helping parents to create a home environment that is aligned with how the school works can help significantly.

The home learning environment includes the physical space and the conditions in which children learn. It is potentially even more important than in a school environment that these two criteria are satisfied. For example, if a pupil has a comfortable space to learn — with a desk, good lighting and lots of soft cushions — but no interest in learning from either parent, then it might always be a battle to get them to do much more than play computer games or surf social media when they should be studying. Schools need to work with parents both to understand their abilities and limitations and to help them create a positive learning environment that works specifically for them and their child. Every family is different so there is no one-size-fits-all approach. This would enable each family to recognise and use relevant learning opportunities in their own home environment, valuing and applying the skills and knowledge that children bring from school into the home and also take back into school.

We can, of course, learn a lot from the COVID-19 lockdowns. As everything moved online because pupils needed to be schooled from home, parents were in the teaching driving seat. As a result, this generation of parents are likely to understand a little more than usual about exactly what, when and how their children learn. There is definitely an opportunity to harness this new-found knowledge before it becomes a distant memory by ensuring that the home environment continues to be one that supports learning. There are likely to be lessons that can be shared with future parents, including how to protect their child while they are learning online.

From our research

How well do parents believe schools support them practically?

Only 18% of parents said their child's school does extremely well at providing practical ideas about how parents can support their child's learning, with 41% saying they do this quite well.

Online

Outcome: *The school creates an online environment where parents find what they need easily.*

This outcome is about more than simply giving parents access to online resources; it is about ensuring that parents are considered when this happens. It is critical that parents are consulted in the development of online resources, so schools can provide what parents need in order to support their child's learning and development, when and where they need them.

Some parents have no alternative other than a mobile device to access school information online. Therefore, the format of the information on your website, portals and apps needs to be chosen carefully, so parents can read important information and be part of your school community. No parent should feel alienated because they do not have a computer or are unable to read small writing that is illegible on a phone, for example.

By first listening to parents and then understanding their habits and skill levels, you can match these with appropriate solutions and achieve your school and pupil goals. It will also guide you in how you introduce new online information, with the right communication, support and even training for parents.

Remember that parents may not access school information online regularly and will forget where to find things. The more intuitive you can make your virtual school environment, the better.

From our research

How well do schools make it easy for parents to find information?

30% of parents said extremely well and 41% said quite well.

29% responded negatively.

Share experiences

Outcome: *Parents are encouraged to share their school experiences to support continuous improvement and learning.*

Quite often in the schools that we work with, parents are discouraged from sharing their views about school in any sort of open forum. Parents may also fear speaking out publicly and being labelled by the school as critical, but mostly because they fear it will have a negative impact on their child.

It is completely understandable that school leaders want to manage the reputation of their school by avoiding damaging comments or undesirable publicity. However, by trying to ignore what may be perceived as negative feedback, issues are pushed underground. Parents will share them anyway through unofficial channels that they have set up themselves, such as via social media or internet forums.

It is much healthier when school leaders create an open, safe and managed environment where parents are encouraged to share their positive and negative views. This will support the school in continually learning, improving and taking proactive action to address and avoid future problems. It will also help you to get a better picture of the themes and trends being discussed by parents, so you can adapt your communications to their needs. Ultimately, openness will build trust in the school.

Critically, school leaders need to ensure that this open and safe environment is school-wide: as well as parents feeling their views are valued, the school team should also be encouraged to speak out and share their ideas and opinions. There should be opportunities for pupils to have their say too. This safe environment should also extend to recognising that mistakes are opportunities for learning. The time and effort invested in creating an environment of mutual respect will be far-reaching and the benefits will show up in all aspects of school life.

Respect time commitments

Outcome: *The school and parents respect time commitments.*

We have seen many schools unintentionally put huge amounts of pressure on parents through either the volume of communications they send home, demands on parents' time to come to the school or expectations to support their children at home. All of these elements are critical to achieving pupil success, of course, but they can also be extreme sources of frustration to already busy, stressed and time-poor parents. As we have already mentioned, schools need to understand the realities of parents' lives in order to develop a true school–parent relationship with pupils at the centre.

For example, if a lot of people in the local community are engaged in the gig economy or do shift work — or, at least, they don't work the same hours as an office worker — the scheduling of school events should recognise this fact. Similarly, bombarding parents with lots of emails is disrespectful of their time, regardless of the job they do; as is asking parents to spend several hours in the evening supporting their children with a specific piece of homework without having given them prior notice. Obviously, this is a two-way street: parents should also be prepared to make time available to fulfil their side of the relationship.

From our research

How well do schools respond quickly when parents contact school?

39% of parents said extremely well and 43% said quite well. 18% responded negatively.

Pillar 3: Culture

Your school's culture is what people experience every time they come into your school, including the rituals, beliefs, customs and social behaviours of your school community. Every school has a distinctive culture or ethos that influences the level of formality, loyalty and general behaviour of the school team and pupils. It can be a powerful foundation for all you do in your school, including how your purpose is lived out every day. An effective purpose-led culture has people at the centre (Humphrey and Macdonald, 2018). Therefore, it must be planned, developed over time and never left to chance. This is why the third pillar of the parental engagement model is culture.

Planned culture

Outcome: *School leaders build a planned school culture that supports parents, pupils and the school.*

In many organisations, culture is often left to grow organically over time. But a positive culture doesn't just happen; it is at its best when shaped and nurtured. Don't forget that a parent's experience of school, as well as their upbringing and environment, will have a profound impact on their willingness to engage with the school. If they had a bad experience of school they may pass this on to their own children. If their own parents didn't get involved with their education they won't know what being involved in their child's education looks like. They will need both practical help and the motivation to change their perspective.

To implement a productive parent–school relationship based on our four pillars of the parental engagement model, it is likely that you will need to instigate a cultural shift that supports a more inclusive role for parents. This starts by understanding what type of culture you want to shape at your school. This will need to be a focus for your senior leadership team, but can be co-created through discussion and research with the wider school team. For example, do you want a culture of mentorship, community and teamwork? Or a culture that is more competitive and rewarding of high achievement? Or a culture that is innovative and progressive? Your culture should support your vision and help you to stand out positively from the schools around you.

We will discuss how to take a planned approach to creating your culture in Chapters 3–7, but your collective values should be the foundational elements of your culture.

These values should change very little over time and should be embedded in everything you do. They are likely to include elements such as trust, listening and recognition. These values should be reflected in your policies, communications and daily interactions. They should be demonstrated to parents through the behaviours of the school team and guided by statements such as, 'We recognise parents who are doing a good job in supporting their children' and 'We listen first'.

Trusted relationships

Outcome: *The school supports the building of trusted relationships between the school team, parents and pupils.*

Trust takes time to develop, but it can be broken instantly. It is the foundation for all good relationships, so creating a school culture that supports the cultivation of trusted relationships is a critical step in breaking down the barriers that may exist for some parents. Schools should take the lead in building trust; expecting parents to take the first step is unrealistic.

Trust can be demonstrated in a number of ways, such as being open and honest, doing what you say you will do, appreciating others, having faith in others and listening with empathy. Importantly, you need to do these things consistently – or almost all of the time. Trust is also fostered when parents' needs are put at the heart of the school–parent relationship. For example, parents who have had negative educational experiences often need the most support. To build trust with them, and to ensure they receive the encouragement they need, may mean going a step further than what might normally be expected – perhaps by meeting with them away from school to reduce their anxiety. When you have built trust consistently over time with parents, you have effectively created an imaginary bank of trust, so if and when something minor does go wrong, you can maintain the relationship by being open and honest and taking swift action to remedy the situation, and thereby avoiding the erosion of that trust.

The key here is perseverance on the part of the school. Building trusted relationships takes commitment through consistent and transparent actions, such as listening to and acting on feedback from parents and making it clear that their input into their child's education is valued and welcomed. Ensuring that school leaders are visible to parents, and accessible when required, are both part of developing trust and demonstrating listening.

From our research

Which school activities do parents appreciate?

We asked parents about the activities that schools organise to build relationships and help parents to support their child's learning.

The most helpful school activities to support parents with their child's learning were parents' evenings: 39% of parents said these were extremely helpful and 41% said they were quite helpful.

The next most helpful activities were opportunities for parents to meet teachers and tutors, which 31% of parents said were extremely helpful and 47% said were quite helpful.

Pupil performances for parents were extremely helpful for 27% of parents and quite helpful for 50% of parents. These, along with parent learning activities, parent forums and parent portals appear to be untapped areas of potential for building trusted relationships.

Parent associations appear to be less of an opportunity, with 23% of parents saying they were not helpful.

Respect

Outcome: *The school team understands and respects parents' beliefs, culture, expectations and parenting style.*

We have already mentioned school demographics. It is equally important for schools to understand the cultural characteristics of their school community. As school leaders move between schools and best practice is applied in different regions, it may be surprising to find that a successful approach in one school may not work in another due to cultural or regional differences. It is therefore important that the school team truly understands how different cultures and beliefs impact on how parents engage with the school.

According to the British Muslims for Secular Democracy (2010: 5):

Parents and educators need to be aware of cultural sensitivities, and there needs to be mutuality and reciprocity of respect. Too often the traffic has been one way with parents expecting schools to respect their traditions and also expecting never to be called upon to respect the traditions of others, to compromise for the greater good.

Ultimately, both parents and teachers share one goal; to provide the best education for children.

Researchers Hal Holloman and Peggy Yates (2013) studied the topic of respect among teachers and pupils. They determined that respect is mutual but that adults generally lead by example. When adults give respect, they get it back in return. When adults show respect to young people, they not only believe in themselves but also those showing them respect. The feeling of value and acceptance is reciprocal.

Involvement

Outcome: *The school supports parental involvement in initiatives and bodies.*

Creating a school culture that is welcoming and supportive is an important step in breaking down the barriers that may exist for some parents. According to a PTO Today survey (see Cosgrove, 2018) of school volunteer leaders, getting parents actively involved in supporting the wider school, beyond their own children, is one of the biggest challenges schools face. Volunteer numbers are falling year on year (Cosgrove, 2018). Parents will resist volunteering for a number of reasons, including not wanting to get sucked into a black hole of endless involvement that will consume an increasing amount of their free time, simply not having the time due to other commitments and priorities, or because they don't feel worthy or good enough.

Giving time to school is possibly the ultimate measure of active parental engagement, so it should be carefully nurtured to ensure that parents are fully supported, respected so they don't get overloaded, and recognised so they feel valued for their contribution to the school. School leaders should also recognise that contributions and involvement from parents are complex; it is perhaps one of the most challenging aspects of school leadership and management. It will not necessarily be consistent in and across schools or in relation to individuals. The key here is perseverance on the part of the school.

Togetherness

Outcome: *The school involves pupils and parents together.*

This outcome brings all of the others together: it is when the school–parent relationship, with the pupil at its centre, really comes alive. We discussed in the introduction the positive outcomes for pupils of family-based initiatives such as FAST. What we are suggesting here is that schools need to adopt a new mindset about how pupils are involved.

It could be argued that old ways of thinking considered home and school to be completely separate. Historically, most schools had an autocratic approach. They didn't see a need for pupils to be actively involved in decision-making beyond learning as instructed, and pupils had no expectations for this either.

However, since the development of the internet, the modern reality is that young people are more connected to the world around them than any previous generation. They have grown up in an 'on demand' world where answers can be found on Google instantaneously. They can watch and listen to what they want, when they want. And most items can be ordered online for next-day delivery with just a few taps of a smartphone. They expect to have an opportunity to influence decisions that affect them, which pre-internet generations did not.

Similarly, schools have evolved from being purely autocratic to being more collaborative, giving pupils the opportunity to contribute to decisions that affect them. A simple example of this is the almost universal implementation of a pupil council at most schools.

This new mindset requires schools to think well beyond the traditional structured parents' evening once or twice a year where progress is cursorily discussed. Instead, it requires an ongoing and school-supported three-way discussion – even going as far as involving parents in setting goals for pupils which they then support them to work towards. Rather than simply asking parents to provide textbooks or other learning materials, they may participate in discussions with teachers about the skills and knowledge their children will require in their chosen subjects.

A further step is workshops for parents about the whole-school initiatives their children are involved in – for example, sessions on topics such as the growth/fixed mindset or mindfulness can help parents to support their children at home. One teacher in our research stated: 'Generally, when the support from parents is there, the pupil thrives. If parents visibly disengage in front of their children, it takes a long time to build a strong relationship; it is near on impossible actually.' Remote learning during the COVID-19 pandemic has provided a fantastic opportunity to involve pupils and parents together. Digital platforms like Google Classroom and Microsoft Teams have enabled schools to share examples of good work, offer praise and post comments on pupils' work.

As one of the key stakeholders, it is vital that parents are involved in decisions about their child's education. Training and information to make the most of those opportunities can be provided as part of managing the ongoing relationship between school and home. This approach ensures that parents' values and interests are heard and respected, as well as creating a level of accountability for the school to its community rather than simply to itself.

Pillar 4: Communication

According to Charles Riborg Mann (1918: 106–107), 85% of our success is related to our ability to communicate. This includes how well we connect with those around us, build relationships and work with others. It determines the quality of our daily interactions and, ultimately, individual happiness and success. This is why communication is the final pillar of the parental engagement model. Parents will almost certainly not always like your message, but they will remember how it made them feel through the way in which it was communicated.

School–home communication needs to be taken seriously – it must be valued, recognised and supported by schools and education systems. It is essential to provide teachers and school leaders with education and training programmes to prepare them to communicate effectively and connect with families in an approachable manner. It is equally important to empower and encourage families to communicate effectively with schools.

Regular and simple

Outcome: *Parents receive simple and easy-to-access information that is clear and consistent.*

The delivery of straightforward school communications to parents requires a planned approach across the whole school. This will involve recognition of the essential communication events which should take priority over everything else, as well as processes and procedures to ensure that parent communications are not simply delivered by the teacher who is able to press 'send' first.

It will also recognise that all parents are different and will want to receive information in different formats and have options to review this in advance of key school events. School communications should be personal without having to be sent individually, frequent without becoming spam and culturally sensitive at all times.

Messages should use language that parents can understand, by which we mean not only plain and simple language but also avoiding the use of jargon, school-specific phrases and abbreviations that are meaningless to many outside of education. An issue not often mentioned due to its sensitive nature is that, in an inclusive school with higher than average numbers of pupils with special educational needs and disabilities (SEND), a significant proportion of the parents may also have SEND but may not acknowledge it. This makes clear and easy-to-access information even more important.

From our research

How well do schools provide parents with the information they need?

31% of parents said extremely well and 46% said quite well.

23% responded negatively.

Listen first

Outcome: *The school is focused on listening to parents and pupils.*

It would be extremely narrow-minded of any school to believe that they don't need to listen to their school community. That said, many of the schools we have worked with haven't had a systematic and planned approach to listening, and there certainly wasn't a principle to ensure that every communication always had a clear feedback loop.

Parents must have the opportunity to ask questions when they are unsure or require help. They also need a voice in order to suggest ideas to help the school improve. Managing questions, feedback and ideas can feel overwhelming for schools, but it doesn't have to be. Listening to parents should be an open-ended process that saves time in the long run.

It is relatively easy today to capture instant responses to both online and in-person events using simple technology. Not only do such tools offer great opportunities to gather feedback, but they also make for a more engaging event for parents, which is more likely to retain their full attention than one where there is no ongoing interaction. For example, apps such as Mentimeter (www.mentimeter.com) or AhaSlides (https://ahaslides.com) have cost-effective packages for educational settings. A slightly more expensive option, which includes the facility to add a leader board if you are holding a quiz, is Vevox (www.vevox.com). It has education-specific prices as well as a free plan. For each app, you need to set up your questions in advance of the event. The app will generate a QR code that parents can scan using a mobile phone or tablet and then respond to the questions as they appear on their device. Afterwards, depending on the options you have selected, you can download and analyse their responses for trends or hotspots, all captured in real time.

If you are not yet ready to interrogate a live audience in this way, good alternatives include Facebook polls, simple questions asked at parent events or gathered through focus groups, or a more formal survey.

From our research

How well do schools listen to parents' ideas and questions?

20% of parents said schools did this extremely well and 55% said they did it quite well.

25% responded negatively.

Training

Outcome: *School team members are appropriately trained in communicating confidently with parents.*

The scope of this outcome can be wide-ranging. It will be governed somewhat by budget, location and the demographic of your school community. We believe that training is necessary to ensure that your school team are able to take an inclusive and confident approach to communication that considers the diversity of their audience — for example, taking into account parents who may have a form of disability, come from a different culture or country, or simply recognising that everyone is different and likes to receive and process information in their own way. It should also include basic guidelines in terms of communicating effectively in person with parents, support for times when there is a need for a challenging conversation or managing parents through changing circumstances. As one school team member stated during our research: 'I work in the independent sector. Parents and their expectations — pastorally and academically — are my biggest challenge.'

Support

Outcome: *The school supports parents to communicate with their children.*

Generally, being a parent comes without training, including on how best to communicate with children. However, some schools offer parenting classes with guest speakers, while others help parents with specific phases of their child's education and stages of life, such as puberty. Although there is a clear line between the responsibilities of school and the responsibilities of parents, there are plenty of opportunities to help parents apply some of the teaching and engagement techniques teachers use daily with children.

Every family is different, so there is definitely no one-size-fits-all approach to this outcome. However, there are common elements to managing communication with children that apply to most families, underpinned by individual support based on the specific needs of each family. For example, training parents for just one to two hours to teach their children reading skills appears to be more than twice as effective as encouraging parents to listen to their children read (Sénéchal and Young, 2008). If you are able to quickly and easily identify parents who would benefit from such support, then you could deliver a simple and impactful intervention to them.

From our research

How effective are parents' evenings from a school team perspective?

From our research with school teams, parents' evenings were seen as the most effective parental engagement channel. Average attendance at parents' evenings ranges from 70% to 90%.

Parents' evenings are still a staple of the British school system, although they can often be a painful tick-box exercise for both teachers and parents and an experience in complete humiliation for pupils! Often teachers operate like a GP, calling in a procession of parents and pupils using a strict time limit to ensure they fit everybody in — and yet still failing to keep to schedule by around the third appointment.

Recognition

Outcome: *Parents are recognised and feel valued for their great work.*

Parents are rarely recognised for their hard work in raising their children or supporting their learning and development. In our research, 51% of parents felt valued by their child's school for supporting their child's learning; 21% stated they felt undervalued and 28% expressed no preference for either. Parents need to know that you value them and their opinions. Our research with parents ranged from perceptions of 'It's a relationship of mutual respect' to 'I don't feel the school trust me to know my son best and take my concerns and comments seriously.'

Our research showed that at least 30% of parents are fearful of school, often based on negative personal experiences. They also have wide-ranging views regarding what a successful school experience will look like for their children. For some it is purely about achieving high grades, whereas others consider success to be a happy and well-rounded child.

Schools need to communicate with parents in ways that resonate with them. They also need to recognise and value them not only for their great work in encouraging their children's learning (in and out of school), but also for their support of the school's goals and ethos. Parents are the primary educators of their children and the way they engage with the school will have a lasting influence on their children's attitudes and achievements.

At the same time, however, there is also a need to recognise when parents are not doing enough to support their children's learning. There is a tendency not to discuss this directly with parents in most schools. This is particularly relevant when parents expect the school to be totally responsible for their child's education and don't recognise the important role they have to play too.

Chapter 2

Where Are You Now?

In the previous chapter, we shared the four pillars of the parental engagement model and the outcomes you should expect to see in each area. In this chapter, we will help you to understand where you are against each of the pillars, and in Chapters 3–7 we will move on to providing practical actions you can take to close the gap between where you are now and where you want to be to achieve your parental engagement goals.

Based on our years of experience of working with organisations to help them resolve their communication issues, we always recommend starting by building an understanding of where you are now. This is because most schools will make assumptions about what parents want and need, and these assumptions may not always be correct. We call this 'listen first', although it is about much more than listening.

Here is a real-life example of why listening is so important within a school context. At a secondary school we were working with in the south of England, the head teacher was hearing reports that parents were frustrated with the school website, and as a result they were sharing their views on an unofficial Facebook page. This was causing lots of unnecessary and unwanted negative publicity, as well as additional work for members of the school office. Consequently, the head decided that the school needed a new website, which was a significant investment of both time and resources. After several months of development, and to much fanfare, the new school website was launched. After some weeks of it being live, the head was still hearing comments second-hand that parents were complaining and there were still flurries of comments on Facebook.

So, what went wrong? Did the new school website miss the mark? Were parents just ungrateful? Or was it, perhaps, that the school had not actually understood the problem in the first place, and as a result the new website was not the right solution? This is what we mean by listening.

We have seen it all too often: a leader wants to resolve a perceived problem, but has not identified the actual problem. In the example above, the problem was that parents wanted more opportunities to share their views and couldn't do this through any of the 'official' school communication channels, so they did so elsewhere. If the head had taken a listen first approach, they would have understood that parents were frustrated because the school wasn't giving them a voice through a formal school forum. It is always important to fully understand your starting point, so you can invest time, effort and money in making focused changes where they will have desired and measurable parental engagement outcomes.

Carrying out your self-evaluation

A relatively simple but extremely effective starting point is to do a self-evaluation of your current position regarding parental engagement. This should be led by a member of your senior leadership team, working alongside your school business manager and others to support the required steps. It will involve drawing on data from within your school, listening to your school community (and to what people are saying online) and looking outwards to learn from other schools.

Step 1: Use your school data

Initially, look at your own school data. You can start with obvious questions such as:

- What is the attendance rate at parents' evenings?
- Do parents attend more optional parents' events?
- What is the level of response when you ask for parent volunteers?
- What response rate do you achieve for important messages where action needs to be taken (e.g. giving consent for activities)?

Also consider data related to the following areas that will also be impacted by levels of parental engagement:

- Pupil results.
- Pupil behaviour.
- Level of pupil absences.
- Attendance on optional school trips.
- Teacher retention/turnover.

Step 2: Check the fundamentals are in place

You can also consider fundamental questions such as:

- Do you have a single person who is responsible for building parent relationships?

- Do you have a clear focus on what you want to achieve in terms of parental engagement?

- Do you have a clear and consistently delivered plan to help you achieve your parental engagement goals?

- Do your school team have a consistent view of what you want to achieve in relation to parental engagement?

- What works well in terms of parental engagement? What has worked less well?

Step 3: Listen to your school team

Next, we recommend that you listen to your school team, parents and pupils in the areas of knowledge, environment, culture and communication, as outlined in the four pillars model.

On pages 46–47 we have listed a set of questions to ask your school team, as a survey or in person, based on these four areas. You should carry out the self-evaluation with different members of staff to provide a fully representative and inclusive view, based on their experience of parents and the issues that are raised on a regular basis.

If you use the questions as part of a survey, we suggest that you adapt the questions so you can ask participants to rate their responses, as well as giving them an opportunity to provide further free-form responses (as required). For example, instead of asking: 'Do parents know what is expected of them to support their child's learning?', ask: 'To what extent do parents know what is expected of them to support their child's learning?' (where 1 is no knowledge and 5 is fully informed). You could use a tool such as SurveyMonkey (www.surveymonkey.co.uk) or Google Forms (www.google.co.uk/forms/about), which will allow you to analyse the responses simply and easily.

Knowledge

1   Do parents know what is expected of them to support their child's learning?

2   Do parents understand the positive impact they can have on their child's learning?

3   Do parents know how to access the technology you use to communicate?

4   Do parents know how their child is doing at school?

5   Do parents know whom to contact at school if they have questions?

Environment

1   Are parents happy to come into school to meet with teachers to support their children's learning?

2   Do parents know what a home environment to support learning looks like and how to create it?

3   Can parents easily find out information about their child or the school using the technology provided by the school?

4   Are parents encouraged to share their school experiences to support continuous improvement and learning?

5   Does the school consciously respect parents' commitments when asking them to support their children's learning?

Culture

1   Do you have a school culture, values and behaviours that support parental engagement?

2   Do you have trusted relationships between school, parents and pupils?

3   Do you sufficiently understand parents at an individual level to provide them with support based on their needs?

4   Do you have a high level of commitment from parents to support school-based initiatives and bodies?

5   Do you involve pupils and parents in a holistic approach to parental engagement?

Communication

1   Does your school provide simple information to parents that is easy to access?

2   Does your school team listen and respond to feedback from parents?

3   Do you provide communication skills training, learning and resources to your school team?

4   Are parents supported in communicating about school with their children?

5   Are parents recognised and do they feel valued for their efforts in supporting their children's learning?

If you ask these questions in person, or simply want to delve into survey responses in more detail, you may find the following focus group checklist helpful. Focus groups should be high energy, open and engaging sessions where people can come together in a safe environment to share their views. They usually enable you to understand more about what individuals are thinking and feeling than a simple survey, as you can 'sense' more meaning from the tone of their responses. This allows you to take actions that will respond directly to real issues and opportunities, rather than assuming what people are trying to say from more closed questions.

Focus groups also provide an opportunity to see who is really passionate about a topic, and therefore who may be a good supporter or even help to make certain actions happen. They can also help you to spot those individuals who might be vocal in not offering their support, but may simply need a further one-to-one conversation to turn them into a persuasive advocate for your parental engagement approach.

Checklist for running a successful school team focus group

Before the focus group:

● Be clear on why you are running the focus group and understand your outcome as it relates to improving parental engagement – for example, to explore the school teams' views on the main challenges related to parental engagement, opportunities to build relationships and the actions you should take.

- Ensure you have full support from your senior leadership team and ask them to actively encourage participation.

- Identify the right people to join so you have a range of opinions and perspectives.

- Choose a time and place that will work for the attendees. Find a 'safe' room with comfortable chairs where people can speak freely and will not be overheard. Offer refreshments if possible.

- Invite people with plenty of notice and give them some points to think about prior to the session, so they have time to reflect and consider their ideas.

- Develop a series of open questions focused on achieving your outcome.

- Ideally have a flip chart and ask someone to help you facilitate the session, so one of you can lead the discussion and the other can write notes.

- Send a reminder for the day before the session to ensure that everyone is clear about the details and attends.

During the focus group:

- Ensure you are ready in the room with all the equipment and your notes in plenty of time.

- Start the focus group by welcoming everyone and explaining that this is a safe and open conversation and you would like them to share their thoughts freely.

- Provide a context about why you are running the focus group and how this will support your school in building stronger relationships with parents (e.g. because these are fundamental to pupils and your school being at their best).

- You can then start the discussion using your prepared questions.

- Create a warm and friendly environment, thanking individuals for their input as they share their thoughts.

- Ensure that people do not talk over one another and that quieter members of the group can speak (without putting them uncomfortably on the spot) – for example, you could say, 'Would anyone who has not contributed yet like to share their thoughts?'

- End your focus group on time and explain what will happen with the input and when the team will hear more.

After the focus group:

- Aim to write up the notes from the focus group within 48 hours, while all the thoughts and comments are fresh in your mind.

- Identify trends, themes and obvious areas for action or further investigation.

- Contact everyone who attended the focus group and thank them again for their support and ask for their ongoing support with parental engagement.

Your school team will be able to provide anecdotal information about parents that will help to inform your engagement approach. This is important because parents' ability to actively engage with school, regardless of how well you implement the four pillars parental engagement model, will be affected by demographic factors such as the type of jobs they have, their level of education, the languages they speak, their income, their family history and many other factors. If your parental engagement framework is designed for people who work typical office hours (e.g. Monday to Friday from 9am to 5pm), but your school is in an area where shift or evening work is common, simple elements like the times of your parent events or the methods you use to communicate may be horribly misaligned.

Below are some suggested areas that you may want to ask your school team about, supported by census information, to understand your parents. However, there may be other areas you want to investigate that are specific to your school or area.

Identify a member of staff — perhaps someone from your school office — who can speak to your school team and gather census data that will give you a simple overview and help you to understand the challenges and motivations for different groups of parents. This information should be recorded and used carefully (some data may be sensitive) to guide your parental engagement approach.

You can find a more detailed parent characteristics workshop called 'Understanding parents school team session guide' at: https://fit2communicate.com/fourpillarsbook.

About parents

1   Types of jobs held by parents and what challenges and/or opportunities this could present when engaging with them (e.g. working in the evening, their views of education).

2   Where parents are located and how this may help or hinder engagement (e.g. those with children who travel a long way to school versus those who are more local).

3   What languages they speak and aspects of their cultural background that should be considered when communicating with them.

About their hopes and fears

Consider carrying out a new parent survey or parent group discussion where new parents talk to existing parents (where appropriate) as an opportunity to really listen first. Alternatively, you could simply ask new parents the following questions when they come into school or when meeting with teachers:

1   What are your hopes and fears for your children?

2   What are your expectations of the school?

3   What would encourage/be obstacles to you engaging with the school?

4   What would encourage/be obstacles to you supporting your child's learning?

You could continue this listening approach by asking members of the school team to volunteer as parent listeners. In this way, they can bring feedback and ideas back to the school team on a regular basis, rather than just waiting for formal listening opportunities.

Step 4: Listen to parents

How you decide to listen to parents depends on your time and resources. You could send out a survey with questions and multiple-choice answers (adapted from the questions suggested on pages 51–52), which is easy to do and relatively straightforward to analyse (if done electronically). However, it only provides one level of information.

As with listening to your school team, you could learn more about the survey results by holding a parent focus group where you ask further questions and dig into the details. This will give you richer and more useful information, so you can take action in ways that will have a positive impact on parental engagement.

You could also choose to focus on one area at a time by asking a question on your website or social media platforms or at parents' evenings. You can find more information about these approaches in Chapters 3–7.

What follows is a list of questions that we recommend asking parents related to each of the four pillars of the parental engagement model.

Knowledge

1   Do you know how to support your child's learning?

2   Do you understand the positive impact you can have on your child's learning?

3   Do you know how to access the technology we use to communicate?

4   Do you know how your child is doing at school or how to find out?

5   Do you know whom to contact at school if you have questions?

Environment

1   Are you happy to come into school to meet with teachers to support your child's learning?

2   Do you know what a home environment to support learning looks like and how to create it?

3   Can you easily find out information about your child or the school using the technology provided by the school?

4   Do you feel able to openly share your school experiences to support continuous improvement and learning?

5   Do you feel that the school respects your time when asking for your support?

Culture

1   Do you believe that the school supports parental engagement?

2   Do you have trust in the school?

3   Do you feel individually supported?

4   Do you feel able to get involved with school-based initiatives and bodies?

5   Does the school involve you and your child sufficiently?

Communication

1   Is school communication simple and easy to access?

2   Does the school encourage you to share feedback and respond appropriately?

3   Do you feel that school team members are able to communicate with you effectively?

4   Do you feel supported in communicating about the school with your child?

5   Do you feel recognised and valued by the school when supporting your child's learning?

Step 5: Listen to pupils

Pupils, particularly at secondary level, can usually articulate exactly what they need from their parents and school to enable them to succeed. It may be as simple as their parents providing quiet time and a space at home to study or being asked how their day went. Parents and schools may assume that parents become less influential as children move into secondary school, but our experience and research indicates that pupils believe their parents' interest and involvement in their learning will help them to be successful.

Parents may feel pushed away by teenagers or ill-equipped to support them as school subjects become more complex. They may not know what to do to support their own child and need clear guidance. When they hear what is needed in the words of their own children, they tend to be more motivated to act than if they are simply told what to do by the school.

Consider gathering feedback from pupils across different year groups, either in focus groups or via a survey. Below is a list of questions that we would recommend asking related to each of the four pillars of the parental engagement model.

Knowledge

1   Do your parents know how to support your learning?

2   Do you believe your parents have an impact on your learning?

3   Do your parents know how to access the technology we use to communicate?

4   Do your parents know how you are doing at school or how to find out?

5   Do your parents know whom to contact at school if they have questions?

Environment

1   Are your parents happy to come into school to meet your teachers?

2   Are you able to study at home?

3   Do your parents use the technology the school provides?

4   Do your parents have a positive view of the school?

5   Do your parents have time to support your learning?

Culture

1   Do you believe the school involves your parents?

2   Do you think that your parents trust the school?

3   Do you feel your parents are supported by the school based on their needs?

4   Do your parents feel able to get involved with school-based initiatives and bodies?

5   Does the school involve you and your parents together sufficiently?

Communication

1   Do your parents find school communication simple and easy to access?

2   Does the school encourage your parents to share feedback and respond appropriately?

3   Do your teachers communicate with you and your parents clearly?

4   Do your parents talk to you about school?

5   Do you think your parents feel valued by the school for the role they play in helping you?

Step 6: Research your school online

If you type your school name into Google, what comes up? What happens if you add words such as 'parent views' or 'feedback'? If you are feeling brave, include words such as 'bullying' and 'residents' to see if anything surprising comes up. This might feel like a strange thing to do, but keep in mind that parents — and, most likely, prospective parents — are going to do this, so it is useful to know what they might find. If you are a school leader, it might even lift a veil on some interesting comments you may not have seen before.

Parent views, and therefore how they feel about and engage with your school, are heavily influenced by what they hear about it in the news and from others. Put yourself on the front foot and be ready to address any negative points with facts as they arise. While you may not have time to do so regularly, it is a good habit to have a member of the school team monitoring the internet, beyond your official social media platforms such as Facebook or Twitter. There are too many channels to monitor individually, but you could set up an automated Google alert to flag when your school is mentioned (go to https://www.google.co.uk/alerts).

When you have gathered various pieces of content from across the internet, take a step back and consider how this information might make parents feel about your school. Look for any trends or themes that come through repeatedly. You may find that there are some persistent commenters with whom you could have a conversation to understand their point of view. This task should be delegated to a member of the school team to undertake as part of their main role, rather than someone doing it at the end of the day as an additional task. Consider this research as another critical part of the listening process and of managing risk and reputation.

This information, along with what the school posts on your website and social media platforms, is what will help to form parents' initial impressions of your school or reinforce those they may already have. If you haven't done so previously, ask yourself whether how you talk about the school and its ethos is being reflected in what you and others are saying online. If not, then it might be time to revisit this. We discuss this topic in our first book, *How to Build Communication Success in Your School: A Guide for School Leaders* (Dempster and Robbins, 2017).

Step 7: Learn from others

If your school is part of a multi-academy trust or similar school partnership, you should be coming together to discuss your parental engagement challenges and, at a minimum, sharing solutions. Even if your school is a stand-alone school, you should reach out to colleagues in other local schools and discuss common challenges around engaging parents. They are likely to be working with a similar demographic so there should be learnings to be had on both sides. Quite often, in our experience, such meetings tend to focus heavily on either the curriculum or operational aspects, when it is the less tangible elements that schools would really benefit from discussing.

You should also aim to attend conferences or events, particularly those that take place online which you can join from school, often dipping in and out as suits your agenda. There are many school-focused events with fantastic speakers sharing expert knowledge and experience gained from working across lots of different schools. These events might feel like a luxury, but if you are selective about what you attend based on the topics being covered, it can be a great opportunity to learn about good practice.

Bring together what you have learned from your self-evaluation to develop insights

Once you have completed a self-evaluation with your school team, listened to parents and pupils, researched your school online and developed a robust understanding of your parent audience, you are ready to bring together what you have learned to develop some conclusions.

We recommend that you capture the common areas and trends from your research into a SWOT (strengths, weaknesses, opportunities and threats) analysis. This will help you to draw out insights from the information you have gathered and start to develop your parental engagement plan. Strengths and weaknesses focus on things that are within your control, while opportunities and threats are less within your control but have an impact from the external world.

On page 56 you will find a simple SWOT template including some suggested examples. There are no right or wrong answers, as long as you base your input on evidence and accurate information.

Strengths	Weaknesses
● Active parent association. ● Regular parents' evenings. ● Parent education events. ● Parental engagement survey/ pulse check.	● No single person who coordinates parental engagement. ● Poor attendance at parent events. ● Parent information in various places.
Opportunities	Threats
● Part of a group of schools, so we can learn from others. ● New head teacher with good reputation for parental engagement.	● New schools in the area that may attract parents/pupils. ● Ofsted parent survey shared negative parent feedback.

Strengths are areas you want to keep and use for the benefit of other areas. Weaknesses are areas you should seek to remedy or at least close the gap. Opportunities are areas you should look to investigate and build upon. Threats are looming storms, so you must understand and prepare for these quickly.

Ideally, a member of the school team should be appointed to oversee this process. They must be supported by the senior leadership team, though — otherwise the actions will not happen. Your SWOT analysis should bring your listening together in one place and will help you to shape where you want to be. We will help you to refine this in the next chapter.

Case study: Taking a planned approach to parental engagement at John Henry Newman Catholic College

John Henry Newman Catholic College is a secondary school in Birmingham with over 1,300 pupils.

What was the challenge or opportunity?

The team recognised the importance of parents being engaged and supported to work in partnership with the college to support pupil learning. However, there were a number of challenges.

Over time, the school had developed a range of messages related to their vision, mission and values, some of which were lengthy and difficult to remember. The number of different words had led to confusion among parents who weren't clear about what was expected of them or what the school stood for consistently. The school needed to be able to explain succinctly the school's purpose and values in everything they did, whether this was at parent events, teacher meetings, presentations, in the school newsletter or on the website.

There was also an over-reliance on face-to-face interactions and no clear way forward in terms of how to use digital tools to communicate with parents. Importantly, parents needed to understand why their role was important in their child's education and how to play their part. They needed to know what support was available and to be guided in how to use this.

What actions did the school team take?

The school recognised that they needed to consult externally in order to make the necessary changes. They worked with specialists to create a three-year parental engagement strategy, consisting of bite-sized steps, in order to engage parents and boost pupils' learning.

They also set aside time to think through the school's purpose and why they wanted parents on side. This has been developed into a clear plan that is supported by the principal and several key individuals to ensure that it happens. Daniel Harvey, strategic director for learning and communication, recognised the importance of having more than one person involved to make the parental engagement plan work, and that these needed to be people who fully understood the power of the parent–pupil–school relationship. He says:

The college needed to first clarify the precise nature of the college mission, how that could be clearly and accurately articulated by all staff and how parents could be engaged. Once this was established, the college was able to use a range of channels to speak to parents and involve them fully in their child's education. Investment in this regular communication has meant that when communication is urgent, parents pay attention and respond quickly.

Daniel works closely with Ben Clayton, head of digital communications and IT for the school. Together they have been able to ensure that electronic communication is fast, efficient and effective.

About the results

The college is now directing parents, in a softly assertive way, by explaining what a parent's role is and why it is important. This has involved being more upfront about the significance of home on pupils' development and learning. They have also provided the support (the how) so parents can make this happen.

Parent handbooks and study guides have been (and continue to be) developed from the perspective of not only the school, but also on understanding the needs of parents in supporting home learning and study. The key is making these easy to read and use, reducing the obstacles so that they can be accessed by anyone.

The team's understanding of parents' needs enabled them to make quick decisions around parent communication related to COVID-19 lockdowns — for example, developing a Friday newsletter, a daily prayer, head teacher video messages and online assemblies.

The school has introduced new technology, such as ClassCharts, which enables them to communicate with parents. They can also see who has and hasn't read messages. This knowledge and ongoing listening helps to inform future parental communications.

The school has also reviewed its website with parents (both current and prospective) in mind, and will continue to develop it as a hub for school information and support.

John Henry Newman Catholic College is on a journey and will continue to build strong relationships with parents. Importantly, the team know where they are going. They have started their journey with a clear plan, so this can be delivered consistently and sustainably.

And this is what the parents say:

I have enjoyed receiving the weekly assembly and having the virtual principal assembly. It's a lot more personable. This is a big improvement on previous years.

Great contact throughout COVID-19.

I hope that the Twitter page will continue. It has been very valuable during the lockdown period.

Chapter 3

Where Do You Go From Here?

Building your parental engagement plan

You should now understand what active parental engagement is in relation to your school, parents and pupils, why it matters and how you are doing with regard to the four pillars of the parental engagement model. In this chapter, we will introduce you to lots of ideas and activities to try out under each of the four pillars.

Before we do so, we want to encourage you to consider exactly what active parental engagement means for your school and in the context of delivering your parent promise. If you don't have a parent promise or think it needs a refresh, please consult Appendix II on how to workshop your ideas.

To kick off your thinking around active parental engagement, we believe that it is about *building trusted and long-term relationships between schools, pupils and parents, through mutual appreciation, respect and proactive and empathetic communication, which enables pupils to be the best versions of themselves.*

We are assuming that if you are reading this with a level of overall responsibility for parental engagement, then you are most likely a member of your school's senior leadership team. However, what follows should not just be the responsibility or remit of just a single person, but rather the whole school leadership team. It is therefore critical to get your leadership colleagues on board to support and lead on the parental engagement plan. They should get involved as early as possible and stay involved throughout, demonstrating progress against your plan and being clear about what role they need to play to ensure it is successful.

To win their support, focus on areas that will support the delivery of your school business plan, such as improvements in behaviour, results, community relationships or parent participation in supporting changes. For example:

- We want to engage parents to activate pupil learning.

- It is proven that pupil outcomes and school morale improve as a result of:

  - ▼ Influencing pupils' perception of school through their parents.

  - ▼ Forming positive, trusted alliances with parents as advocates for the school.

  - ▼ The school team better understanding family dynamics and culture.

  - ▼ Changing the dynamic into an ongoing conversation about learning.

  - ▼ Providing opportunities to build parent confidence so they can help pupils to learn.

When the support of the senior leadership team has been secured, you can then proceed with the following activities. Without their support, any ongoing activities are going to be extremely difficult to sustain, so it is critical to take the time you need to gain support from your leadership team.

Create your school's definition of parental engagement

You might like to develop your own description of active parental engagement to share with the whole school team, parents and pupils. Here are some simple steps that your school leadership team can follow to create your own definition, one that will resonate for your school and guide you to where you want to be.

1   Focus on what you want pupils to achieve — the mindsets, capabilities and skills — guided by your school values and purpose.

2   Consider what challenges you face as a school and local community that are influenced by parents — for example, do pupils have low aspirations because their parents have low aspirations, or are they overly competitive due to very high parent expectations?

3   Understand what is and is not working right now for each party — parents, pupils and the school team.

4   With all of the above in mind, what would active parental engagement look and feel like from your perspective?

5   Create a one-sentence statement (like the example on page 59) of what active parental engagement means for your school: *We believe that active parental engagement is about …*

6   Test it with your wider school team to ensure that it is inspirational and makes sense to others.

When you have your school's definition of parental engagement, identify what this means for what you do every day as a school team. In other words, what sort of behaviours and actions are needed to support this definition and enable you to bring it to life in your school community?

We have defined six behaviours that relate to our definition (see page 59) to help you pinpoint your own behaviours:

1   **Value differences.** We put ourselves in the shoes of others in order to recognise and understand their motivations and challenges, so we can benefit from our differences inclusively and without judgement.

2   **Demonstrate appreciation.** We proactively show appreciation of others for their important role in supporting pupil learning and development, even before a child starts school.

3   **Communicate inclusively.** We communicate simply and with consideration for the needs of others, recognising that their requirements may be different to ours.

4   **Listening to understand.** We listen to others first, ensuring that they have a voice and feel valued.

5   **Build trust.** We constantly look for ways to build trust by doing what we say we will do, recognising when we may not get it right and taking action to rectify it for the future.

6   **Work together.** We respect others in all we do, acknowledging that we all have a common goal which is to support pupils to be their best.

This is a great opportunity to rethink the desired relationship between school and parents, with pupils at its heart. Consider how your school creates a great parent experience and demonstrates that it values parents in ways that are significant for them. This means meeting parents on their own terms – physically and emotionally – and considering their personal circumstances, values, beliefs, customs and limitations.

Define your strategy with measurable goals

The next step in developing your parental engagement strategy includes considering where you would like your school to be and when, defining what active parental engagement will look like at each stage and setting measurable goals.

Where you would like your school to be and when

Take some time to consider exactly where you would like your school to be in one, two, three or more years in terms of active parental engagement. Think about specific outcomes rather than simply aspirations. For example, if you want stronger relationships with parents, why exactly do you want this? What outcome do you want to achieve?

Alternatively, you may want to create a stronger community where parents take on a more active role in assisting your school team. You may want to support pupils in their learning, with a greater focus on results and them being at their best. You may want to take the pressure off the school team, who are taking on responsibilities that need to be reinforced at home — for example, around behaviour management or attendance. You may want to change the perception of your school in the community by nurturing supportive parents who will tell the real story about your school.

Develop a clear parental engagement outcome and associated actions for each year, building on the previous year, to enable you to achieve your goals. For example:

Year 1: Put the foundations in place

- Develop a school environment where parents feel welcome.
- Better understand parents' needs.
- Develop communication principles.
- Agree your consistent messages in terms of what you want to provide to parents and what you need from them.

Year 2: Build on the foundations

- Ensure your school team is trained to communicate with parents.

- Recognise parents who make a great contribution to pupil learning.

- Put in place fully planned, coordinated and two-way parent communication.

- Measure and improve based on what you learn.

Year 3: Create sustainable actions

- Create increased opportunities for parent voice and enrichment.

- Ensure your values and vision are lived through parent interactions.

- Support parents in speaking as advocates for your school.

- Continue to measure and improve.

Define what active parental engagement will look like at each stage

When you know where you want to be, you can define clearly what you want active parental engagement to look and feel like for your school. To support this, and to hold yourself and the rest of your school team to account, set some SMART (specific, measurable, achievable, realistic, timely) goals. Your short-term goals should be stepping stones to your longer-term goals.

For example, a short-term goal might be to better enable parents to support pupil learning at home through a targeted information campaign that will cover the reasons why their support matters, as well as what they can do practically. This could be achieved realistically within a six-month timeframe, as a stepping stone to the longer-term goal of creating supportive parents who will speak positively about your school with others in the local community. Building trust and relationships takes time. It is not an ad hoc event but should be consistent in everything you do, every day and over the long term.

Set measurable goals

You will need to measure your progress against each goal, so make sure you have taken this into account when you set them. For example, your campaign of enabling parents to support their child's learning at home might have a measurable target of 75% of pupils reporting that their parents have spent time supporting them in a specific area, or for 80% of parents to say they have the information they need to support their child's learning. You might choose to have a year-on-year target for the percentage of parents who say they feel welcome when they visit the school, starting at 50%, increasing to 75% and then 90%. Or you might decide to set a target for how confidently the school team communicate with parents.

You should also consider what measures will indicate whether your parental engagement strategy is working. For example:

- Pupils leaving due to dissatisfied parents (and why).

- Parents attending school events.

- Parents who volunteer to help.

- Parents who would recommend your school to other parents.

- Parents who feel confident in supporting their child's learning.

The goals you set for active parental engagement at your school, and how you measure them, should be a discussion for the senior leadership team. If the goals are going to be more than a wish list that ends up in a metaphorical bottom drawer, they should be integral to your school development plan. There should also be clear and collective ownership across the senior leadership team, who should all be accountable to your governing body.

As part of the process, it is a good idea to set some short-term goals that will provide evidence of progress and keep everyone engaged and inspired. For example, over the coming term you could commit to reviewing the new parent pack and updating it with feedback gathered from parents who have used it.

Here is an example of a three-year parental engagement strategy:

2021–2022: Establish the foundations	2022–2023: Strengthen the foundations	2023–2024: Be the best in class
Outcomes:	Outcomes:	Outcomes:
• Defined parent personas. • School information management systems and mindsets in place. • Defined and consistent school messages. • Basic and planned parent support approach and sessions established to outline expectations. • Measures and baseline established (school development plan). • School team have training to support the above.	• School values and vision are lived through parent interactions. • There are increased opportunities for parent voice and enrichment. • Parents who make a great contribution to pupil learning are recognised. • School team has training to support the above. • Continued measurement and learning.	• A school environment where parents feel welcome. • Parents speak as advocates for the school, inside and outside of school. • Parent communication is planned, coordinated and two-way. • School team have training to support the above. • Measure improvements and learn (school development plan).

Define the activities to make your strategy happen

Based on your self-evaluation and parental engagement definition and goals, you are now ready to define the activities you want to take.

You should pinpoint where you need to improve in the areas of knowledge, environment, culture and communication. We have provided lots of activities to help you close the gap, between where you are now and where you need to be, later in this chapter. You do not need to do every activity. Simply focus on the pillars and activities that will support you most in improving and building on your current strengths.

Before we start to look at ways to help you achieve your outcomes, let us consider two final areas that you will need to focus on in order to implement your active parental engagement strategy.

Identify owners and allocate responsibilities

You will need to give overall responsibility to someone for the delivery of your strategy. This will normally be a senior leader with an appropriate level of authority to ensure that the actions are delivered, and who will report back regularly to the school leadership team and governing bodies. This person should be the main point of contact for all parental engagement activities, but they should not work alone. They will need to be supported by other school team members, including senior leaders.

If you have a team or registrar focused on recruiting pupils, they will need to work seamlessly with those members of your team who manage the relationship with parents during the time pupils are on roll. They will need to jointly support the delivery of activities to achieve your parental engagement goals, so that you can make good on the promises you made to parents and pupils when they started at your school.

Ideally, each activity needs an owner and to be tracked in terms of the progress or support required to make it happen. You can find an example activity plan in Appendix III. We would recommend that you consider enlisting the support of a group of parental engagement champions from different areas of your school. To recognise the power balance in the relationship, this should include school team members, pupils and parents. Your school team champions can help to ensure that actions happen in different parts of the school, building support and feeding back what they hear from the wider school community. They will also bring energy and enthusiasm, have the confidence to talk about the importance of active parental engagement and have their ear to the ground.

Set dates to review progress against your plan and celebrate successes

Before you start, schedule dates to review progress against your plan using the same self-evaluation approach you undertook at the start. Aim to learn from what you have achieved so far, check that your goals are still realistic and celebrate your successes — no matter how small they may seem.

However, you don't have to wait for each formal review point to gather feedback. For example, you can have informal discussions with the school team and parents about progress against specific outcomes, use feedback opportunities such as polls and short pulse surveys, or ask open questions on your Facebook page or other social media platforms. Importantly, recognise the progress you have achieved so far in order to stay motivated and energised on your journey to active parental engagement. If you don't, it is easy to feel overwhelmed by how far you still have to go.

Activities to help you achieve your parental engagement goals

In Chapters 4–7, we have provided strategies focused around the four pillars. For example, in your self-evaluation you may have identified that communication is an issue, so refer to the activities under the communication pillar (Chapter 7). Always focus on the activities that will work best for your school, because every school and its circumstances are unique.

Chapter 4

Pillar 1: Knowledge

Area for development: Parents, school team and pupils know what is expected of them in the partnership

Activity summary:

- Develop a written agreement between school, parents and pupils.

- Make it realistic, clear and relevant.

- Ensure all parties can discuss and buy into it.

- Refer back to the agreement regularly.

- Support your school team in bringing it to life.

- Engage pupils.

Develop a written agreement between school, parents and pupils

Develop a written agreement between your school, parents and pupils that sets out expectations for all sides of the relationship. This should include minimum 'must do' actions and then 'if you have time' options, indicating what support the school will offer parents and pupils to make these happen.

Make it realistic, clear and relevant

Many parents will simply not be able to do more than the 'must do' activities. Ensure that these are set at a sufficient level to deliver the parent side of the engagement equation. Parents should not be judged for *only* doing the minimum, and neither should those who do more receive favourable treatment. It is simply about recognising that every family is unique and treating them accordingly. Nevertheless, you should feel able to openly inform and/or challenge parents when their lack of support for their child, or the school in general, is hindering their child's progress. An example parent–pupil–school agreement that can be personalised for your school is available at https://fit2communicate.com/fourpillarsbook.

Ensure all parties can discuss and buy into it

The next stage is critical: you must ensure that parents and pupils buy into it and truly understand what it means to them. There are a number of ways you can do this.

- **Email parents at the start of the year.** The easiest option is to send the agreement by email to parents, encouraging them to discuss and agree this with their children. However, this isn't a very engaging strategy and busy parents are unlikely to give it more than a quick glance. Therefore, you need to obtain confirmation from parent and pupil that they agree to support it, either through signing it or some form of online acknowledgement.

- **Share a personal video message from your head teacher.** A more engaging option that is likely to both grab parents' attention and drive action would be to share a personal video message from your head teacher which speaks directly to parents and pupils about their role, especially to the parents of new joiners.

- **Use existing parent events.** It may be possible to use your first face-to-face parents' event of the academic year to reinforce these messages directly to parents. If you are lucky, you might be able to enlist some ex-parents to record a message, or even speak in person, about how they supported their children and the difference it made.

Top tip: Always make it a conversation

Whichever approach you use, make sure it is not all one-way communication from school to parents. Encourage parents to share their views, concerns or questions in open (and safe) forums, such as a closed Facebook group or through your website. Appoint someone to manage responses in a timely manner (or do so on a shared rota basis) to ensure that parents feel listened to and can see action as a result of their feedback.

Refer back to the agreement regularly

It is not enough to share the agreement once. You need to regularly remind parents and pupils of their commitments at appropriate times. For example, you could have the agreement to hand at parents' evenings when they are discussing the progress of their child or if there is a behaviour related incident. You could even display a summary of the agreement in corridors where parents and pupils are likely to be waiting.

Support your school team in bringing it to life

The school team must be supported in appropriately challenging parents and pupils who aren't fulfilling their side of the agreement. You could include a link to a standard version of the agreement on your website and in the footer of every email you send to parents. You could also share case studies and other examples from your school which serve as reminders to parents that engagement is not just the responsibility of the school.

As mentioned at the start of this book, parental engagement should be formalised as a fundamental aspect of the school team's responsibilities by making it part of your annual performance objectives, along with specific, measurable targets. This provides a good opportunity to discuss ideas about parental engagement and get feedback as part of the process. Consider timetabling the topic as part of a group discussion, either at an all-school team meeting or an INSET day or departmental meeting. The key consideration is to agree, rather than impose, targets and actions; they need to be realistic as well as measurable.

Engage pupils

Many schools already have a pupil agreement or pupil promise that learners sign up to when they join. However, you can take this a step further and include them in the parent–pupil–school agreement so that they have an explicit shared responsibility for parental engagement, such as encouraging their parents to attend parent events.

It is easy for pupils to neglect this obligation, so make it real for them. For example, you could run a fun interactive session with pupils at the start of term, where you ask them to share ideas about how to get their parents more actively involved in the school. You could then give them follow-up materials to discuss with their parents at home, with a view to bringing ideas and actions back into school for further discussion. To encourage pupils to discuss topics with their parents, you could organise a competition or set up a points-based rewards system. Obviously, this needs to be considerate of and accessible to all parents.

Area for development: Parents know why, when and how to support their children's learning

Activity summary:

- Provide evidence and inspire parents about why their support for their children's learning is important.

- Provide a clear calendar view of when parents need to support learning, so they can plan ahead.

- Help parents to understand the minimum (and additional) actions they need to take, perhaps reinforced by fellow parents who can share their experiences.

- Involve pupils so they can assist their parents.

Inspire parents to want to support their child's learning

In earlier chapters, we have explored the reasons why parental engagement is important. The evidence shows that there is a clear case for the positive influence of actively engaged parents, but parents need to understand this in terms that resonate for them individually. If you talk to parents about their child achieving better grades then, of course, many of them will be inspired by that outcome. However, there will be some parents for whom higher grades are not the ultimate goal. As demonstrated in many of the FAST initiatives, the benefits of family learning stretch beyond simple academic benefits to enhanced social and behavioural skills. Add to this a mindset of continuous learning as a result of family-driven values, and it is clear that understanding each parent's 'why' is a critical part of active engagement.

Top tip: Start with your why

In *Start with Why*, Simon Sinek (2011) asks why some people and organisations are more inventive, pioneering and successful than others, and why they are able to repeat their success again and again. He argues that in business it doesn't matter *what* you do; it matters *why* you do it. According to Sinek, this philosophy is what drove people like Steve Jobs, the Wright brothers and Martin Luther King. The premise is to start with why and be inspired or inspire others.

In terms of our parental engagement model, isn't having parents inspired and inspiring others exactly what we are seeking? Of course it is! So, it makes absolute sense that parents know why active parental engagement is so fundamental to the success of their children. It is not a magic formula; in fact, it isn't even a secret formula. According to Sinek, it is a proven formula.

The first outcome of our model covered some ideas for sharing what is expected of parents with regard to their active engagement, and this should go hand in hand with explaining why their active engagement is so important. If your school is sending details to parents by email, sharing an engaging video or holding a virtual meeting, don't just tell parents what they need to do, tell them why. Communicate with them in their language too, avoiding educational jargon, internal school language and acronyms that parents simply won't and shouldn't be expected to understand.

If your school team is able to interact with them in person — for example, at parents' evenings, either virtually or face to face — teachers should skilfully ask them to describe their hopes and dreams for their children and how they expect their children to achieve them. This will allow the school to understand the 'why' on parents' own terms. It is much more challenging than sticking to the same script every year, but it is a great way of demonstrating that the school is listening to parents and wants to understand them.

Have a planned and clear calendar view for when you need parental support

Develop a simple parental engagement calendar, based around the traditional school calendar, that summarises for parents when extra support will be required (in addition to ongoing support), such as at exam times. Aim to fit it on a single page (as in the example on pages 74–75), highlight critical periods and share it with every parent at your school. The school team could print it out and refer to it when speaking with parents at events such as parents' evenings, but you could also initiate specific communications that remind parents when hotspots are coming up and their support will be even more crucial.

Parent calendar — when we really need you to support your child in 2021–2022

PARENTS

These shaded blocks indicate when your support for your child is essential.

NOVEMBER: Mock exams

MARCH: Start of revision period

JUNE: Exam period

	September					October					November					December				
Monday		6	13	20	27		4	11	18	25	1	8	15	22	29		6	13	20	27
Tuesday		7	14	21	28		5	12	19	26	2	9	16	23	30		7	14	21	28
Wednesday	1	8	15	22	29		6	13	20	27	3	10	17	24		1	8	15	22	29
Thursday	2	9	16	23	30		7	14	21	28	4	11	18	25		2	9	16	23	30
Friday	3	10	17	24		1	8	15	22	29	5	12	19	26		3	10	17	24	31
Saturday	4	11	18	25		2	9	16	23	30	6	13	20	27		4	11	18	25	
Sunday	5	12	19	26		3	10	17	24	31	7	14	21	28		5	12	19	26	

	January						February					March					April				
Monday		3	10	17	24	31		7	14	21	28		7	14	21	28		4	11	18	25
Tuesday		4	11	18	25		1	8	15	22		1	8	15	22	29		5	12	19	26
Wednesday		5	12	19	26		2	9	16	23		2	9	16	23	30		6	13	20	27
Thursday		6	13	20	27		3	10	17	24		3	10	17	24	31		7	14	21	28
Friday		7	14	21	28		4	11	18	25		4	11	18	25		1	8	15	22	29
Saturday	1	8	15	22	29		5	12	19	26		5	12	19	26		2	9	16	23	30
Sunday	2	9	16	23	30		6	13	20	27		6	13	20	27		3	10	17	24	

	May						June						July						August/September				
Monday		2	9	16	23	30		6	13	20	27			4	11	18	25			1	8	15	22	29
Tuesday		3	10	17	24	31		7	14	21	28			5	12	19	26			2	9	16	23	30
Wednesday		4	11	18	25		1	8	15	22	29			6	13	20	27			3	10	17	24	31
Thursday		5	12	19	26		2	9	16	23	30			7	14	21	28			4	11	18	25	1
Friday		6	13	20	27		3	10	17	24			1	8	15	22	29			5	12	19	26	2
Saturday		7	14	21	28		4	11	18	25			2	9	16	23	30			6	13	20	27	3
Sunday	1	8	15	22	29		5	12	19	26			3	10	17	24	31			7	14	21	28	4

Share the specific actions you need parents to take

When it comes to explaining 'how', recruiting some ex-parents who are willing to share their experiences can really help to make it real for new parents. While there are some minimum actions that parents can take, such as providing a suitable space for children to learn at home and reading their progress reports, sharing experiences of what worked and what didn't from those who have already been through the school experience will certainly help other parents to avoid making the same mistakes. With all of the 'why', 'when' and 'how' elements, explaining once at the start of the year is unlikely to be sufficient to keep most parents interested and engaged. Use planned school communication, such as regular and end-of-term newsletters or events, to remind parents of the basics — as well as adding new and simple opportunities.

Schools that cater for children with special educational needs do a great job of explaining to parents why, when and how to support their child. We have seen some fantastic examples in our work with schools. As we saw in the introduction, the team at Ashmount School share videos with families to support homework via YouTeachMe. This allows the school to provide personalised messages for the children to listen to at home with their parents and forge stronger home–school relationships. Small-scale models enable a deeper relationship to develop between schools, pupils and families which may not be practical in larger secondary schools. However, the approach leans heavily on the FAST principle of being in it together which is relevant to all schools. We also advocate joint discussion, where the school listens to the parent and vice versa, because the evidence demonstrates that it makes a significant difference to levels of engagement.

Involve pupils to ensure they have the support they need from parents

Bringing pupils into the school–parent relationship can offer huge benefits to all parties. In the first years of secondary school, before communication between young people and their parents becomes more challenging as a result of puberty and advanced learning, pupils can be encouraged to have family discussions about why they need their parents' support. Empowered pupils can even be encouraged to negotiate a support agreement with their parents. Not only is this a great way of involving them in the process of developing a supportive three-way relationship, but it also gives them an opportunity to develop wider skills, such as negotiation, influencing and planning.

Ahead of pupils negotiating support agreements at home, you should inform parents about what this will involve and make it clear that their child will be expected to lead the discussion. To follow up and learn from this activity, ask pupils to share their outcomes and ideas with their peers at school. You will need to carefully manage this approach to ensure that children who aren't able to have a discussion with their parents still feel included, perhaps by creating an ongoing dialogue about what is meant by parental engagement which involves all the pupils.

Area for development: Parents are able to use school technology, including portals, apps and tools

Activity summary:

- Put yourself in the shoes of parents — understanding what they may find challenging or useful about your new or existing app, portal or other school technology.

- Create a reason for parents to want to use the technology.

- Provide the support, communication and training parents need.

- Monitor whether people are using the technology and adapt your approach.

Our recommended four-step approach to introducing school technology to parents is available at: https://fit2communicate.com/fourpillarsbook.

Put yourself in their shoes

Schools are often keen to introduce technology, such as apps, to support parental engagement. From the school's perspective, this can be a one-size-fits-all approach which makes it easy to post updates to parents in just a few taps. From the parents' perspective, however, this can be a barrier if they don't have access to a smartphone or can't use the app for another reason. The introduction of any technology must be carefully thought through and managed to ensure that parents joining your school can access it and know how to use it. Aim to consider what might motivate parents to use the technology and what might be an obstacle.

Create a reason for parents to want to use the technology

The next step is to create the desire for parents to want to use the technology by explaining what is in it for them. It is important to put their child at the centre of your communication campaign and explain why it will help their learning and development.

Top tip: Remember that people need to rewire their brain in order to create new habits

It can be easy to underestimate what is required to ensure that human beings want to change and do something differently — in this case, using your school app or online portal. It literally requires them to rewire their brain. Remember that people either need something better to move towards (a simpler way to do something with a better result) or the current situation needs to be so uncomfortable that they seek out new ways to make their lives easier.

Provide support, communication and training

You may want to offer online or in-person sessions, where parents can ask questions about how to use the technology or you could share a video talking parents through how to use it.

Engage parents through both communication and training, while also listening to ensure they understand and are taking the right actions — and helping them along if they are not. This would apply both to the introduction of new technology at your school or to new parents joining your school, and using your technology for the first time.

Off-the-shelf user guides are not always the most accessible way in for parents. We recommend that, as a minimum, schools review standard materials before sharing them with parents.

Monitor whether people are using the technology

You may choose to monitor the usage of your app or online portal via built-in analytics and data. In addition, if you have a group of parent champions (or simply friendly parents whom you can ask for feedback), invite them to use the technology first. Listen to their feedback on what guidance would help them so you can develop a tutorial that is specifically aimed at your parents. Continue to ask them to share feedback from other parents so you can adapt how you support them and achieve the maximum return on investment from your technology-based tools and resources.

Case study: Supporting parents through a virtual learning environment from Frog[1]

Frog is an example of a virtual learning environment (VLE) that supports parental engagement and builds stronger relationships with parents as part of the wider school community. Frog is a leading education technology provider with a unique approach to delivering practical solutions for schools and educators worldwide. Their technology gives schools the ability to adapt, change and personalise based on what they need.

Historically, parental engagement through VLEs has been focused on attainment, attendance and results. The more enlightened schools then started to survey parents and ask them what they wanted to see when they logged on to the VLE parent portal. As a result, parental engagement in terms of VLEs has evolved alongside other technology such as apps, email and text.

Providing parents with attendance, behaviour and attainment results can often be more of a stick to hit pupils with than something useful. Frog finds that parents are far more interested in seeing what their children have done at school — the work

---

1   See https://www.frogeducation.com.

itself, be that photographs or videos – and enabling the parents to 'like' and comment on the work. This not only engages the parents, but also provides an authentic audience for the children and can increase the discretionary effort they apply to the work they do.

Parent communication has expanded during the COVID-19 pandemic to include a focus on mental health, well-being, and how to structure the school day and support teaching children at home. It has been the route to ensuring that pupils attend their virtual classroom – supporting parents as teaching assistants.

Schools utilise VLEs in different ways – for example, some use them to book trips and activities, share trip information and forms, and even photos from the event itself. Alongside good analytics and data, they want instant push notifications and to know who is engaging with what. Other schools are more advanced in their thinking and use e-portfolios to support learning around a particular subject and share it with parents and their child. Parents and pupils can take photos, record audio and video and add it to the e-portfolio. This empowers children in driving parental engagement, taking control of their learning and sharing this with their parents. VLEs can also support areas such as admissions, attendance, school clubs, dinners, payments, extracurricular activities and parents' evening bookings.

During COVID-19, some classroom teachers were tasked with creating online learning resources. These were uploaded and available on the VLE. Teachers, pupils and parents could all see what they should be doing and when, and the analytics showed which children were engaging with the lessons.

Some schools have started incorporating support for pupils' mental health and well-being into their VLEs so parents can recognise and look for signs, as well as being aware of what pastoral care is available and what action to take. Frog has seen some great examples of innovative teaching during the pandemic. For example, one school used the Frog classroom resource and 'beamed' the teacher into the middle of a page.

Secure pages in Frog enable an experience similar to Facebook, Instagram and Pinterest, allowing young people to connect through social media, supporting relationships with friends and reducing isolation while studying at home. Frog also provides a voice for parents – for example, on major topics that require consultations such as a school converting to an academy or changes to school meals.

Frog believes, as we do, that it is fundamental to help parents understand how to use the VLE from the start. The VLE is introduced to the school team first, then to pupils and finally to parents. Some schools just send out a letter, but the best way to bring parents on board is to share the VLE at a parents' evening or event, show them how it works and then let them try it out.

Area for development: Parents know how to access and understand their children's progress information

Activity summary:

- Understand how parents prefer to access their child's progress information.
- Share the information before important progress conversations.
- Be creative and engaging in how you share progress.

Understand how parents prefer to access progress information

The relationship between school and parents is an ongoing learning journey — where parent feedback helps the school to shape the best way to share progress information, for example. It is important to continue to listen, while also managing expectations around what you can and can't change. Clearly, you can't cater for every different parent preference, but there are some basic considerations that will help you to assist parents in taking important actions to understand targets or grades and support their child.

For example, mobile technology is a great way to share bite-sized information with parents or make information accessible to them on a regular basis. However, as mentioned previously, digital technology won't work for every parent, so it is important to consider parents' preferences and provide alternative options where possible. Speak to parent groups or friendly parents to find out how they would prefer to access information, ensuring that you take an inclusive approach and considering groups of parents with different needs.

If your school is using an information management system (such as SIMS, Engage or iSAMS), you have the opportunity to provide parents with an inside view of how their children are doing. These platforms can usually give parents a much clearer and more detailed picture than many will get from their children. Not only do they enable progress to be shared, but they also work as a one-stop shop for parent messages from the school. They allow schools to monitor how active parents are on the platform, giving you a better understanding of whether there is actual parental engagement or not. For schools without such sophisticated technology, parents may only get real feedback at set intervals during the school year — at parents' evenings or end-of-term exams being two obvious examples.

Share progress information before important conversations

Share progress information with parents in advance of formal parents' evenings and ask them to review it ahead of the meeting. This means that time with the teacher can be focused on discussing the strengths (or weaknesses) of their children's work. It is also a respectful way of recognising that some parents prefer to have time to review information before discussing it. If parents are given a sheet of numbers to read through during their biannual five minutes with the teacher, many will find it difficult to digest the information immediately and translate it into questions or concerns.

Be creative and engaging in how you share progress

Some schools share ad hoc feedback about progress through postcards from teachers or tutors, usually celebrating good work or attitudes to learning. These can be time intensive to write and manage, but boost parental engagement as well as making pupils feel good and encouraging them to stay focused.

Top tip: Put the pupil at the heart of all communication

The opening sentence of almost all parent communications should be, 'Your child's learning …' or similar. The child is the common factor and motivator for parents and schools, so centring your communication around them will strengthen your message and help pupils to be at their best.

Area for development: Parents know whom to contact for help and when they can expect a response

Activity summary:

- Be clear about who parents should contact with a simple information finder.

- Set standards for when parents can expect a response from school.

- Set up mailboxes for regular or repetitive messages.

Be clear about who parents should contact

Schools are often overwhelmed by parent emails, so there may be a nervousness about sharing direct email addresses. However, by putting some simple steps in place, you can avoid teachers being inundated by emails and having to reply at all hours of the day.

It is important to be clear about whom parents should contact about what topics. Parents may feel the need to email a teacher directly simply because they don't know who else to contact and can't find the relevant information. Parents should be guided to the right points of contact — for example, 'If you have a question about school holidays, please visit this web page' or, 'If you have a concern regarding your child's progress, please contact this person, who will get back to you within a specific period.'

We recommend that you create an information finder for your parents (we have included a template in Appendix IV) which includes points of contact for the most common queries you receive. This will help to reduce the problem of parents not knowing whom to contact or how to do so. It also gives the clear message that your school takes parents seriously and values their role in the school–pupil–parent relationship.

You should share this information directly with parents at the start of each year and again when it is updated. Make it easily accessible for parents on your website too. Remember that it should save your school team time, as they won't have to answer the same questions over and over again, and better manage parent expectations and frustrations.

Set standards for when parents can expect a response

Your information finder should include your agreed service levels — in other words, how long a parent should expect to wait to receive a response. For example, if your information finder includes a key contact for lost property, you need to have an internal process that will ensure that parents receive an (immediate) acknowledgement when they email that address, which would also state how long it will take until somebody gets back in touch with them. There is no right or wrong here: service levels are defined by each school and are subject to internal processes. However, you need to ensure they are realistic and do not damage the school–parent relationship by setting unworkable expectations that can't be realised.

Top tip: Ensure that your school team understands your communication standards

You school team should be fully informed about the service levels, standards and sign-offs required for parent communication. This includes where to redirect messages if they are sent to the wrong person to ensure a quick action or response. Invest time in ensuring that they are confident in what is required so they can support your parent communication consistently.

Set up mailboxes for regular or repetitive messages

You may want to set up mailboxes for your school office or for safeguarding concerns, so that a number of people can access the same mailbox. This will take the pressure off a particular individual. We also recommend that you have a mailbox for urgent emails, with a clear guide as to what constitutes urgent. A parent may struggle to get through to school by phone on an urgent matter, so it is good to have an alternative mailbox that is monitored regularly and avoids urgent emails being lost in a sea of daily school messages.

Chapter 5

Pillar 2: Environment

Area for development: The school team creates a school environment that welcomes and supports parents

Activity summary:

- Ensure buildings are well signposted.
- Make your school welcoming, with a simple message when parents arrive.
- Train reception staff to create a friendly and supportive first impression.
- Be respectful of parents' time through good meeting etiquette and general standards.
- Provide guidelines to support your school team when engaging with parents.

Ensure buildings are well signposted

Our model defines the school environment as the physical surroundings and the non-physical conditions. Now, we do recognise that school buildings vary greatly both in terms of how old they are and where they are situated. That said, there are still common physical aspects that each school can control.

For example, school buildings should be appropriately signposted. Parents' evenings are usually well covered, with pupils acting as guides, but when parents go to school for other reasons, try to make sure they feel just as welcomed by friendly signage. While pupils will quickly remember their way around the school, parents who visit only once or twice a year are more likely to get lost, especially if they are having to make a quick, unplanned trip due to an unforeseen incident. You should aim to make their experience as painless as possible.

A welcoming message and environment for when parents arrive

Depending on your school's demographic, a nice touch to create a friendly environment for parents and pupils is to have welcome messaging in the various languages that represent your school's demographic. Make sure the parents' waiting area is a pleasant place to be — consider displaying pupils' work or achievements, especially if it is away from the main reception area. Ensure that your school premises are litter free and anything that requires fixing or is out of order is kept out of view.

Top tip: Ask someone to give you their impressions

Ask someone who hasn't visited your school to walk around with you and share what they observe, feel, smell and experience. Encourage them to be as open and honest as possible so you can pinpoint what works and where you could make improvements. A fresh pair of eyes and perspective will undoubtedly support a better school environment.

Train reception staff to make a good first impression

Often, the first non-physical aspect that parents encounter when visiting the school are the people they meet at reception, who, in our experience, are usually extremely skilful and patient school team members. This primary point of contact can go a long way to creating a positive impression for parents. As we have seen, a parent's own personal experience of school may shape their perception of their child's school (our research shows that one in four parents had a neutral or negative experience of school), so encourage the entire school team to make visitors feel welcome.

Respect parents' time with good meeting etiquette

There are a host of aspects related to dealing with parents in both formal and informal meetings that will be specific to your school. However, there is also some best practice in this area that will help to create a positive environment for visiting parents.

Ensure that meetings start on time, particularly when working parents have made special arrangements to attend the school. We are fully aware that teachers can get caught up with unforeseen incidents, so make sure parents are informed if a member of staff is running late rather than just keeping them waiting. Turning up late, without any forewarning, can create a negative impression that parents might read as the school lacking discipline, being disorganised or disrespectful of them.

Then there is the space where the meeting takes place. Obviously, confidential discussions will be held in a private room which should be comfortable and welcoming. Some parents may not appreciate having any type of discussion in an 'open' environment, so it is worth checking with them first (even when time is short) before launching into a discussion in the middle of the school reception area.

You could also consider having an open-door policy for parents at certain times of the day, when the head teacher could invite parents to join them to discuss issues, share ideas and provide feedback. You can find support on having challenging conversations with parents in Chapter 7.

Provide guidelines to support your school team when engaging with parents

When parents are invited into your school — for example, for a parents' evening — give every member of the school team who will be present a pre-briefing (verbal or written) about what is expected of them with regard to how they engage with parents. Make sure they understand that everyone has both conscious and unconscious biases, and that these will affect their interactions. Talk to them about the tone of their communications with parents and how this will influence their experience. You could include hints and tips that will help them to remember some of the little things around how they interact that can make a real difference to how parents feel.

Area for development: Parents understand what a home environment that supports learning looks like and are supported in creating this

Activity summary:

- Communicate your minimum requirements for a positive home learning environment at the start of term (e.g. a home learning guide).

- Involve and listen to parents' challenges in creating a home learning environment.

- Involve pupils in the conversation and find out what support they need.

- Provide additional support for parents (e.g. school drop-in sessions) at important educational milestones for pupils.

Communicate the minimum positive home learning environment requirements

You can communicate information about the minimum requirements for a positive home learning environment to all parents at the start of the year in your initial parent–pupil–school agreement. This should make everyone's role, responsibilities and contributions very clear.

You can support the agreement with a home learning guide for parents (you can find an example at https://fit2communicate.com/fourpillarsbook) which includes:

- The importance of a parent's attitude to learning (and reading) and to be a role model for their child.

- How to talk to their child about their learning and day at school (with age-specific ideas).

- What being an active learner means, so they can support this mindset with their child.

- How to use technology to support their children, both from school and other sources.

- How to share concerns and to be an advocate for their child.

- How to build a relationship with teachers, tutors and the school, including attending events and getting involved with parent groups.

- Other contacts and sources of help for supporting their child's learning and development.

Involve and listen to parents' challenges

The school needs to understand what challenges parents face when creating a suitable home learning environment for their child. Aim to find out what they do to help their child learn and how they overcome personal challenges with motivation and specific learning difficulties. You should gather this information sensitively, recognising that each family is unique and that you cannot possibly understand everything about their home environment.

This topic is a good one to discuss at slightly less formal events, such as open coffee meetings, where groups of parents come together, either physically or virtually, to discuss a specific topic with the head teacher or another member of the senior leadership team or teacher. Avoid any form of comparison between families as this can be perceived as judgemental and may lead to disengagement.

Involve and listen to pupils to understand their needs

Pupils are at the centre of the school–parent relationship, so gather information from them about what they need from the school and what parents can do to support their learning at home. You could do this during personal, social, health and economic education sessions or during tutor times. Based on this feedback, consider providing parents with tips on supporting home learning, such as how to set up an area for focused study, questions to ask to support their child's learning and how to overcome challenging times when their child doesn't want to learn.

Provide additional support at moments that matter for parents and pupils

Offer parent and pupil drop-in sessions around specific milestones, such as how to manage exam revision at home. Focus on both the mechanics of how to make it happen and also how to protect family relationships and get into healthy habits. You could also invite guest speakers with expertise in the area of home learning to offer support to parents.

Top tip: Even older pupils need their parents' support

Even though teenagers may seem to grow away from their parents, it is important to acknowledge the importance of this relationship in a child's development and learning. At this stage, many parents feel concerned about how they can support their growing children when they are struggling to understand the subjects they are learning. Often, pupils just want someone to ask them about their day and show an interest, even though this may not be obvious from their behaviour or response!

Area for development: The school creates an online environment where parents find what they need easily

Activity summary:

● Test what works well and what doesn't in terms of online information by asking parents.

● Provide a simple one-stop shop for everything parents need in one place.

● Provide support, particularly when introducing new tools and resources.

● Consider further opportunities to use online tools to support parents.

Ask parents what works well and what doesn't

Most information for parents is likely to be provided online, so make sure that this is quick to access and navigate — from the perspective of parents, not just the school. Changes to the system tend to occur incrementally, so check in regularly with parents to ensure that your online environment still works well for them and they know where to find your information finder which will point them in the right direction.

Provide a one-stop shop for parents for all online information

Rather than existing in multiple places, information for parents should ideally be a one-stop shop. This could be a web page or simple PDF document (there is an example information finder in Appendix IV) which provides clear links to the various places where parents will find specific information.

Offer support as part of parent events

Offer formal information sessions for parents (particularly those who are new to the school) to both train them in using your school technology and also to understand what they might struggle with so you can provide additional support.

Consider further opportunities to use online tools

During COVID-19, when children had to be home-educated for a number of months, many parents had no choice but to use school prescribed technologies to support their children's learning. Despite the steep initial learning curve, this has accelerated the opportunities for the adoption of digital technology to support home learning, including webinars, online platforms, videos, podcasts and websites. Consider what else you could make available online to enable parents to support their children at home. But don't forget the digital divide: materials should be accessible via a mobile phone as well as a computer or tablet.

Area for development: Parents are encouraged to share their school experiences to support continuous improvement and learning

Activity summary:

- Create a listening environment with regular opportunities for parents to share feedback.

- Run short, regular pulse surveys, with clear benchmarks and targets, to highlight progress and issues for action.

- Hold listening sessions in a safe space with clear rules of etiquette in place.

- Consider a closed, managed online parent forum with simple guidelines.

Create a listening environment

Feedback from parents really is a gift, although it is sometimes difficult to hear and needs to be managed carefully. But wouldn't you rather hear what is on your parents' minds in a way you can action before the next Ofsted visit?

In order to create an open listening environment, you need to build trusted relationships. This starts by creating psychologically safe spaces for parents to share their views. School team members who run the sessions or ask questions need to be guided on being supportive and patient, while sensitively managing any potentially negative feedback. Importantly, if you ask for parent feedback then you need to respond or act based on what you hear. Failure to do so will create mistrust and parents will be less likely to share their views in the future.

There are a number of ways that schools can encourage parents to share their views, both positive and negative, about their experience of being a parent at your school, as outlined below.

Run regular pulse surveys

Short pulse surveys should be run throughout the year – around every three to six months. Try to invite different groups of parents at different times so you don't ask anyone more than once during a school year. Aim to ask at least 50 parents, as a minimum, to give you a representative view of your school parent population. Shorter surveys are easier to administer and analyse than larger ones, and you are more likely to act on the responses, either by addressing any issues raised or sharing why you are unable to act. Also use the opportunity to celebrate positive feedback as a school.

Hold listening sessions

The wider acceptance of virtual meetings since COVID-19 has opened up the opportunity for termly online listening sessions with parents, hosted by a member of the school team. The sessions should offer a safe space where people feel comfortable talking about their experiences as a parent at your school.

Invite parents with a specific topic in mind – for example, solicit their views about the biggest challenges they face in supporting their children's learning at home – so they know what will be discussed and are able to do some preparation and thinking beforehand. Parents will not only share their views but also help each other. For instance, if a parent raises a specific issue around their working hours, another parent might offer a solution. In our experience, this type of open discussion can have benefits far beyond the initial meeting. The parents who attend will speak with other parents about the meeting, explaining that the school asked them to share their views. If, as a result, actions are taken by the school, this will only serve to increase parents' positivity towards your school.

Consider a carefully managed online forum

Another option to encourage parents to share their views is through a closed forum. For example, you could ask for parents who would like to explore a specific topic. When you have some volunteers, invite them to a private forum, such as a closed Facebook group, where you can post specific questions and they can respond. If you choose this option, it is critical that all comments are monitored and acknowledged. Where appropriate, actions based on comments should be taken quickly by appointed members of staff.

Top tip: Ask parents to be your biggest supporters

When was the last time you asked parents to talk supportively about your school to others in the community? It is a simple request that schools may not always think to ask directly, but it can be a green light to encourage parents to share positive feedback and recognise that your school would welcome this action. When you see a parent talk encouragingly, either in person or online, say thank you and let them know you appreciate their support.

Area for development: The school and parents respect time commitments

Activity summary:

- Set times/days for parent events that take into consideration their work and lives, offering different options where feasible to include as many people as possible.

- Create safe and respectful opportunities for parents to talk with school team members, recognising that some parents may dread coming into school.

- If you have asked parents to join you at an event, respect that they will also want to ask questions, so include opportunities for feedback and discussion.

- Support parents in respecting your school team's time using a simple information finder to ensure they contact the right member of staff.

Be inclusive in setting times/days for parent events

Establish a fully inclusive approach for school events that recognises parents' differing time commitments. For example, parent events usually take place after school, so those parents who work shifts or have other childcare commitments may not be able to attend. The same applies to schools where children board.

In our online world, it is possible to make most parent events available remotely for those who missed out – for instance, PowerPoint slides that were shown at the event could be made available on your school website afterwards. However, these offer little context, no sense of dialogue between school and parents, and are unlikely to be very informative. A more inclusive alternative would be for an appropriate member of the school team to spend a few minutes recording a voiceover to the slides, adding explanations and incorporating questions that were raised at the actual event. This may take additional time to do properly, but when the impact of positive parental engagement is so high, it is surely worth it to ensure that every barrier to participation is removed.

Equally, when teachers spend an extra four or five hours in school for parents' evenings, there should be an expectation that parents respect this commitment and make the effort to attend. Ensure that attendance at specific school events is clearly specified in the parent–pupil–school agreement at the start of the school year.

Create a safe and comfortable environment that respects parent preferences

Some people are anxious about coming into school and having to mix with lots of other parents. They may also dread speaking with teachers, however welcoming they are. Consider scheduling private consultations on different days for these parents, so you are inclusive and reach as many of them as possible.

Listen and encourage parents' questions

When you have a parents' event and ask parents to give their time, provide an opportunity for them to have their say and ask questions. Parents should know whom to contact about different topics and understand when they are likely to receive a response. Similarly, parents need to respect your school team, so be clear about event etiquette such as how to ask a question. Any negative feedback should be addressed quickly and carefully.

Support parents in respecting your school team's time

We have already discussed the role of the information finder in enabling parents to make contact with the right person, thereby saving their own time and respecting the school's time.

Top tip: School team meeting guidelines for better meetings

By having a simple set of meeting guidelines, you can save time, ensure people's ideas are heard and respected, and create greater value from your meetings. You can see an example at: https://fit2communicate.com/fourpillarsbook.

Chapter 6

Pillar 3: Culture

Area for development: School leaders build a planned school culture that supports parents, pupils and the school

Activity summary:

- Define the experience you want parents to have of your school, based on your school vision and values and what makes you stand out from other schools – your parent promise.

- Establish the moments that matter for parents and demonstrate that you are delivering on that promise (e.g. their child's first day at school).

- Keep your promise in all you do – behaviour, governance, leadership style, curriculum and so on.

Define the experience you want parents to have of your school

In order to build a planned culture, you need to start by having an agreed vision and values. From a parent's perspective, this comes alive through the experience that they, and their child, have during their time at your school.

When a prospective parent learns about or visits your school, they are forming expectations. These may be implicit or explicit – for example, they may be related to conversations or your website. Whether you know it or not, you are making a promise to them about what they can expect from their child's time at your school.

Rather than leaving this promise to chance, we recommend that you develop and articulate your school promise, aligned to your vision and values, and are clear about how parents and pupils will experience this at your school. This includes many aspects of school life, but there will be significant moments that matter more, such as a behavioural incident or when choosing options.

A clear school promise

Sources of the promise
- Marketing, including website
- PR and advertising
- Word of mouth
- School team recruitment
- Education events

Potential parents, pupils and school team

The promise is delivered consistently

Moments that matter
- Inducting new pupils
- Support through education milestones
- Dealing with school issues
- Leaving school
- School team experience

Current parents, pupils and school team

Trust and advocacy is built

- Parents are visible supporters
- Community support
- Alumni send their children to school
- Staff recommend school as a place to work

Parents, alumni, pupils and school team

Like any promise, if it is delivered consistently, your school, parent and pupil relationships will grow in strength. Likewise, trust and relationships will be damaged if the promise is broken.

We have included an example of how to deliver a school promise in Appendix II.

Ask some members of the school team if they understand the school promise. You are seeking to find out if they recognise what makes your school unique in the eyes of parents and, to a similar degree, pupils. If there is any inconsistency or uncertainty in their responses, the whole school team needs to come together for an open and honest discussion about your school promise. Afterwards, re-share the school promise in writing with them individually and make it visible in the staffroom.

If you don't have a clear school promise, then you have an opportunity to create one with the support of your whole team. Initiate discussions with school team members, initially in small groups, and ask them to come up with what they believe is your school's promise. Bring everyone together to discuss their ideas and agree what promises you want to make to parents and pupils.

Top tip: Deliver on your marketing and external promise

Some schools may have a member of staff responsible for marketing the school to prospective parents and pupils, while others may simply have a website with a page for prospective parents that shares some wonderful words around what the school will do for their child. Whatever promise you make, ensure there is a clear and continuous understanding of how to communicate and deliver on this promise once a child has started at your school. Sometimes parents feel there is a step change when the marketing team or registrar hand over a child and their parents to the school team, who may have different views on how to bring the school's promise to life. This can lead to poor pupil retention over time.

Establish the moments that matter for parents

Once you have agreed and shared your school promise with the school team, you need to cross-check this against day-to-day actions and, more importantly, the moments that matter. These will be the times when parents need you most — for example, open days, their child's first day at school, how you deal with a behavioural issue or how you support their child through their exams. Every child and their parents go through a school life cycle where these moments that matter can be tracked; this is when your promise needs to shine through.

Keep your promise in all you do

Beyond the key moments mentioned above, you also need to live your promise in everything you do. For example, do the behaviours of your school team support your promise? Does your delivery of the curriculum, school governance and approach to pupil recognition reflect your promise? Take a look at your school marketing literature to ensure that your school promise is clear and succinct to anyone reading it. Go back to the listening exercise in Chapter 2 and review whether what is being said about your school by your school team, parents and pupils is consistent with your promise.

Look beyond the present and consider how you can keep your school promise alive. For example, ex-pupils, their parents and school team members who have left could all be advocates for your promise. Offer opportunities for them to stay in touch through social media (in a Facebook group or on Twitter), emailed updates or newsletters.

Case study: Creating a culture of optimism and connecting through humour at Monkton Combe

Monkton Combe School is an independent boarding and day school for boys and girls aged 2 to 18 near Bath, Somerset. It is a member of the Rugby Group of independent boarding schools in the UK. The principal, Chris Wheeler, believes in the power of communication. He has had experience of supporting pupils, parents and staff at times of crisis, which he was able to apply during the COVID-19 pandemic when connecting as a community became even more important.

What was the challenge or opportunity?

When Chris joined Monkton Combe five years ago amazing things were already happening. But the school was a hidden gem and not many people knew it existed. What the school stood for wasn't entirely aligned with reality or where the school team wanted it to be. As a Christian school, they wanted to bring together the Christian community where faith is an accepted part of every pupil's experience.

What actions did the Monkton Combe team take?

Firstly, Monkton Combe has a principal with a slightly different way of thinking. Maybe it is down to his personality or his life experience, but Chris challenges himself and is constantly innovating and adapting. He has experienced school situations unlike many others. For example, six weeks after arriving in Nairobi to take on a head teacher role, disaster struck: the Westgate shopping mall shootings in 2013. The school community experienced significant loss of life and 17 pupils were taken hostage by al-Shabaab militants during the four-day siege.

This became an education in the importance of sharing what little information was known. The school put in place a text message update service to keep people informed as the crisis unfolded. When the siege was over and the school began to think about recovery, Chris invited Terry Waite, who spent 1,736 days (almost five years) kidnapped and chained to the wall in a dark cell in Beirut, to speak with the school community. Terry listened and spoke with pupils and staff.

Chris said: 'Terry Waite talked about the importance of acknowledging the current situation and feelings, drawing on personal experiences and stories to connect with people and then helping them to move forward into the future. These are lessons I have taken through life and have applied in the recent COVID-19 pandemic, particularly around how to manage fear and protect children from fear.'

Chris is also a great believer in the power of humour to bring people together: 'It connects us during good and bad times, and our shared experiences make us a stronger community, so we can keep going together.'

Engaging parents in surprising ways has become a speciality at Monkton Combe. For example, Chris started by questioning why only the parents of prize-winners were invited to prize-giving. He made it clear that they would only hold prize-giving ceremonies if it was a celebration of everyone and everything that happened at the school. The next prize-giving brought together the whole community in one marquee, followed by a picnic on the lawn.

But there was an even bigger surprise for those who attended. After a traditional start to his speech, Chris started a flash mob-style 'Les Misérables' performance that involved many of his school team. The video went viral on YouTube and news stations in the UK and abroad, eventually being screened on NBC News across the United States. It also signalled a change for Monkton Combe. This principal was happy to be human: he was authentic and vulnerable. It broke down any sense of 'them' and 'us' between staff and pupils, and also parents and staff. It allowed people to come together with light and respectful humour as a strong community of which they wanted to be a part.

Chris and the team didn't disappoint at the following year's prize-giving. Once again Chris started in a traditional way, then ripped up his 'same old' speech and ran out of the marquee. He was seen, on a video screen, running around the school and talking with pupils so parents and other pupils could hear about the year's achievements in the words of the children. It gave parents a window into the life of Monkton Combe pupils and connected with parents much more than just a speech from the principal. The school team think that if they are asking the children to put themselves out there, the staff need to do it first. Monkton Combe has a great team who are happy to oblige.

Chris believes in understanding the different communication styles of those around him to better connect with them. This is something we talk about under the communication pillar. He recognises the importance of inclusive communication and respecting and benefiting from people's differences, while also being aware of blind spots. This listening culture is particularly visible in the preparatory school, with a head who relishes feedback. Chris says, 'Catherine Winchcombe loves feedback and strongly encourages it at every opportunity.'

Finally, Chris rethought everything during COVID-19: 'It's not enough to do the same thing online. It's a totally different environment so we have to adapt and do something different. This needs to be fun and draw the community in.'

About the results

The parent feedback speaks for itself:

'In what must have been the toughest year outside of wartime, this school has absolutely thrived. We have a principal who leads from the front and that leadership permeates downstream. Whether it's a spontaneous operetta from the staff, African dancing of the whole senior school or the inspirational letters that make me want to follow the principal's reading list, there is an energy and inclusiveness that has real depth. This is new and very welcome.'

'I truly feel that my children, and all of the pupils that pass through your doors, will leave Monkton believing in their own "limitless potential" and the amazing things that they can be capable of in their lives ahead. This is down to the commitment, support and absolute energy of you and your staff.'

'During this year especially, Monkton has really triumphed in adversity. Above all, my children are happy, but it's also important that they are learning and growing. It's better than it was before.'

'It feels like the culture of the school has changed in a very good way in recent years.'

Area for development: The school supports the building of trusted relationships between the school team, parents and pupils

Activity summary:

- Look for opportunities to continually build trust as a school team, not just the senior leadership team.

- Be as transparent and open in your communication with parents as possible, always putting their child at the centre.

- Show parents that you appreciate the role they play.

- Start as you mean to go on at your school open day.

Look for opportunities to build trust as a school team

You can build trust with parents and pupils by ensuring that the school team takes deliberate actions. This starts by giving trust to others and by thinking the best of them, not the worst. For example, during COVID-19, school leaders who let go of control and allowed their team to manage back-to-school COVID arrangements benefitted from reduced personal stress and an empowered school team. Similarly, a parent who has taken an innovative approach with their child which has resulted in a positive outcome, even though it may not have been the planned way, is likely to stay actively engaged if they feel respected, trusted and valued for doing so.

Trust requires consistent actions every day, so create and share simple checklists for the school team to follow, such as one parent-focused action to take every day. Being vulnerable and human is also a foundation for developing trusted relationships.

School leaders who openly admit that they don't have all the answers are more likely to be trusted than those who attempt to provide an answer for everything.

Keeping promises, no matter how small, will build trust. For example, when parents are kept waiting for school leaders in meetings or in reception, it is often due to a serious issue in the school that could not wait. While unavoidable and unpredictable, leaving people hanging around is a form of broken promise. Make sure that even small promises are honoured, or at least let parents know if something has happened last minute. When promises are broken or mistakes are made, admit to them immediately and propose how you plan to learn and move forward.

Top tip: Adopt behaviours that build trust

We recommend adopting eight behaviours that build trust (Poorkavoos, 2016):

1   Be transparent.

2   Stick to commitments.

3   Demonstrate trust.

4   Be personal.

5   Be consistent.

6   Appreciate others.

7   Listen well.

8   Demonstrate vulnerability.

We believe that the most important factor is being consistent: if you consistently demonstrate these behaviours, you will build trust with parents and others.

Be transparent and open in your communication

Transparent communication, in the sense of not withholding information for the sake of it, will build trust compared to unnecessarily withholding information, which will break trust. Try to be personal and bring some of yourself into your parent and pupil communications. School leaders who created selfie video messages for parents and pupils during the COVID-19 lockdown went a long way to being both human and trustworthy in their eyes.

Trust is built when pupils and parents feel they can talk openly and will be listened to without being judged. Talk about trust, fears and the school culture in general on a regular basis, as part of normal conversations between the school team, parents and pupils, to build a safe environment where everyone feels like they have a voice.

Show parents that you appreciate them

Appreciation is an important element in showing someone that they are valued and trusted. Say thank you and practise gratitude regularly — for example, a daily thank you to a parent or school colleague can make all the difference. Find ways to celebrate individual pupil successes with their parents as they happen, not three months later at the next open evening. Finally, trusted relationships are built on dialogue, so listening to parents and pupils — as covered elsewhere in this book — is critical.

Start as you mean to go on at your school open day

School open days are a great opportunity to give parents a sense of what it is like to be part of the school community. Below are some points to ensure that your open day is the start of a trusted relationship between the school team, parents and pupils, ensuring that your school stands out for the right reasons.

What do you want parents to think, feel and do as a result of the open day?

Be clear on the one message you want to get across to parents and children, but also how you want them to think and feel about your school. What will they say about your school that makes you stand out from others? Where are you innovative? Where do you excel? How are you demonstrating that you are living your vision?

Involve your full team in planning the open day

Ask your team for ideas so the day is created with their full support and allow plenty of time for planning. Develop a whole school theme and approach so there is a clear flow which can be carried through from how you promote the event to the initial head teacher welcome and the classroom activities. Your team should be working together to deliver a consistent message to parents and children.

The open day opportunity starts well before the day

Promote the event in advance through your website, adverts in the local press and on social media. Consider ways to excite people about the open day before they attend – for example, a short (one- or two-minute) video featuring pupils from your school explaining how much they are looking forward to meeting parents and their children, either sent in advance by email to potential attendees if they have pre-registered their contact details or posted on your website.

Ensure everyone is fully prepared

Take time to brief all school staff and pupils who will be involved on the day. Ensure they know exactly what they are doing and how to answer questions. Provide a simple briefing document with helpful information about the tour route, some history of the school and key facts. Avoid making the day too formal. Parents may feel that open days aren't the 'real' school, so the more you can do to make them feel relaxed, the better the outcome – even allowing them to explore the school by themselves if that is possible.

The big opening

If you have a welcome talk at the start of the day, minimise the time the head teacher or other senior teachers speak. They should be engaging and inspiring and include personal stories that connect with prospective parents and pupils. Focus the bulk of the time instead on hearing from current pupils, or even current parents, about their experience of your school.

The grand tour

Taking prospective parents and children around the school is a great opportunity for pupils, but choose children who can do this confidently and ensure they can answer questions confidently.

Show how great the teaching is

Make sure there are practical and fun things for the children to do that showcase your teachers' abilities. Alternatively, you could have actual lessons running that the children can join in with – perhaps science experiments or maths quizzes. Clearly, you want the children to be asking their parents if they can go to your school over any other school!

Ask attendees how it went and keep in touch

Send a short email message after the event to thank parents and children for attending. You could ask them to complete an online survey comprising questions that help you to understand whether you achieved your open day goals. You could also ask staff who were involved for their feedback. Learn from what you hear and improve for the future.

Area for development: The school team understands and respects parents' beliefs, culture, expectations and parenting style

Activity summary:

- Take time to understand parents and offer training to staff, if required.
- Listen to and learn from parents to understand their context.
- Position your school at the centre of your local community.

Take time to understand parents

Building a school culture with parents in mind must include a respect for and understanding of parents as individuals. There may be a need for specific cultural awareness training for school staff if there is a significant gap in understanding. Culture is a partnership and parents have as much of a role to play as the school.

It can take time and effort for members of the school team to learn about unfamiliar cultures. It may require them to challenge their existing beliefs and be empathetic to ensure that the school adopts a fully inclusive approach. However, this work is critical and will create many benefits, including better relationships and a happier and more successful school community.

Top tip: Build cultural awareness through learning

It is easy to assume what parents may or may not think, feel or do based on their perceived backgrounds. Take a look at self-directed unconscious bias and cultural awareness courses online that will ensure your school team are well informed, open-minded and able to build relationships with different parents and pupils. Also consider specialist organisations that can provide specific guidance on the ethnic minority groups in your school.

Listen to and learn from parents to understand their context

Alternatively, you could invite a parent or group of parents into your school to speak with the school team (and pupils, if appropriate) about aspects of their culture. Ask them to share how their culture affects their beliefs and attitudes towards school, how it shapes their expectations and any differences in parenting style. You can further this parental involvement by developing an equity, diversity and inclusion steering group consisting of school team members, pupil representatives and parent volunteers.

Position your school at the centre of your local community

When parents have a good experience of your school and feel respected and valued, they will speak positively about your school in the local community. And if the local community has a positive perception of your school, you will receive greater support and tolerance when you want to do things such as extend your school or if there are behaviour issues.

Below is a checklist to help you think about how to position your school in the local community and to guide you in the messages that you share with parents.

- Identify what you want people in the local community to think, feel and do to support your school.

- Understand the strengths, weaknesses, opportunities and threats related to how you are seen in the community.

- Consider the challenges and opportunities in building community relationships.

- Look at some of the other schools in your local area to understand what they are doing well and not so well, and what you can learn from them.

- Articulate the key messages that you want staff, parents, pupils and the local community to hear and say about your school.

- Create a planned, sustained approach using persuasive (and trained) spokespeople, channels (e.g. community newsletter) and activities (e.g. local media relations development, social media plan, community events) that deliver your desired outcomes, including telling stories about what you are already doing to support the community.

- Develop a network of staff and parent champions who are your ear to the ground and who are happy to reinforce your school messages. Maintain energy and focus for this group through regular updates and suggest simple ways to share their views.

- Measure how your community relations are going in terms of social media, local press, level of complaints and positive comments. Ideally, ask the local community a question or two when there is an appropriate opportunity, or even share a survey at school events.

- Provide regular updates to your school governing body and senior leaders to celebrate success and agree further actions.

Area for development: The school supports parental involvement in initiatives and bodies

Activity summary:

- Invite parents to volunteer and support your school — to benefit their child but also as a personal development opportunity.

- Provide training and resources to help parents become confident and informed volunteers.

- Let parents lead the way in coming together with other parents to create parent groups around natural community topics and things they are passionate about.

Invite parents to volunteer and support your school

In order to support and encourage parental involvement, school leaders need to lead by example. This means being visibly present at school events (not just parents' evenings) which parents are asked to attend and support.

All schools should be bold enough to talk with parents about the benefits of volunteering. For example, as well as learning more about the school, volunteering also offers the chance for personal development and opportunities to learn or hone skills, which come with potential career benefits. It is also a great way to meet and connect with other people, to make a difference to the education of their own children and those of others, and develop a higher profile in the school and wider local community.

Provide training and resources for confident parental involvement

Some parents may be nervous about volunteering, so they will appreciate the opportunity to receive some training. There are several organisations specifically set up to support parents when getting involved with schools, such as Parentkind (www.parentkind.org.uk) and Sharing Parenting (www.sharingparenting.com). There are also specific organisations that can help parents to learn about more formal school roles and provide training, such as the National Governance Association (www.nga.org.uk) and Governors for Schools (www.governorsforschools.org.uk).

It is important to be clear about what you need from parent volunteers and what the role involves at the start, rather than let parents get sucked into a black hole from which they desperately want to escape. Provide parents with access to information from relevant organisations to both help them to become informed and also to reassure them that robust training is available if they do decide to get more involved.

Let parents lead the way – with your support

Have you thought about asking parents to share their ideas about how they might be able to support the school, rather than school driving the conversation with them? For example, one school we have worked with runs a weekly magazine club for pupils. This was initially set up and supported by parents with experience in the area, but it is now self-sustaining and continues without additional parent support.

Top tip: Say thank you and show you value parents

Thank parents for getting involved on a regular basis, not just en masse but individually where possible. Treat parent volunteers like gold dust and show your appreciation through thank you letters from the head teacher or small gestures that create those powerful moments of recognition. But keep in mind that not everyone likes the limelight, so make sure you consider individuals' personalities to ensure your actions are viewed positively.

Case study: Putting school at the heart of the community at Flakefleet Primary School

Flakefleet Primary School is a community school in Lancashire for children aged 2 to 11. Head teacher Dave McPartlin and his team have worked hard to make Flakefleet a place where people feel they belong — whether they are pupils, parents or members of staff.

What was the challenge or opportunity?

When Dave first joined the school, parents didn't come into school very often and he frequently received complaints from parents. He believes that a school should be at the heart of the community. It might be an old-fashioned view, but it was just the approach that was needed. It was an opportunity that Dave and his team grasped with both hands — and the results have been amazing.

What actions did the Flakefleet team take?

The Flakefleet team surveyed parents, asking them what they needed in order to improve their relationship with the school, so that together they could work better to support the children. They invited parents into school to share their views and to break down barriers.

Dave and his team took the findings and set a new tone for the conversation. They introduced fun videos, face-to-face coffee mornings, bingo nights and Flakefest — a big annual event that brings families (around 1,000 parents) and the whole school community together. These events all focus on creating a sense of belonging and enjoyment, where everyone is valued and feels inspired.

The school community has been further strengthened through outreach to families when they needed it most — with food parcels, bedding and other support — both generally and during the COVID-19 pandemic.

When the coronavirus hit, it was difficult to run induction events for new children. However, that did not stop the Flakefleet team. They arranged to visit the children at their homes with small gifts and big smiles. This proactive reaching out — taking school to families — made a huge difference. This approach is likely to continue in the future.

There have also been the appearances on *Britain's Got Talent* which shared the Flakefleet magic with the whole country. It strengthened the support of parents and the local community behind a wonderful group of children and the head teacher and staff who made it possible.

About the results

Staff retention is almost 100% over five years, they have an extra 100 children on roll over the last three years, and there have been significant improvements in teaching and learning and workplace culture — focused on anything being possible! Barriers have been broken down, trust has been built and this has carried the school forward positively in times of uncertainty.

Parents now trust the school to do the right thing. Even when mistakes are occasionally made, they are forgiving because strong relationships have been created. Trust has been built through consistent and continuous communication and supportive actions, driven by committed and passionate leadership. Parents talk to one another and are advocates for the school. There is an immense sense of loyalty and pride that binds the community together and creates better outcomes for the children.

Area for development: The school involves pupils and parents together

Activity summary:

- Create opportunities for parents and pupils to join you at school for discussions in a safe environment where they feel able to speak out.

- Create simple guides and videos for parents so they can practically and confidently support their child's learning.

- Consider community venues (rather than school buildings) for school recruitment or new year start events to help parents and pupils feel more relaxed.

Create positive opportunities for discussion involving parents and pupils

Make sure parents feel involved by offering opportunities – beyond parents' evenings – where they and their children can come together with a school team member for an in-depth discussion about the child, with both school and parents listening. This is an ideal opportunity to gather parental input and agreement and to set individual pupil goals that parents are much more likely to support in the family home.

Also consider how to make the opportunity feel safe from a pupil perspective. It can be fairly nerve-racking when your parents come into school, so many pupils will feel a level of apprehension about speaking out. Reinforce the idea that pupils should speak up and that you want to hear their views, but give them a chance to prepare what they might want to say beforehand.

Provide parent guides, support and videos

Help parents to get involved in specific lessons by encouraging teachers to create simple videos that explain, in easy-to-understand terms, what is being learned to parents. Make these videos available on your learning platform (and give parents access). Suggest enrichment activities that will help parents to build constructive relationships with their child too. Ideas might include science experiments, home DIY projects, family trips to the library, age-appropriate museum exhibitions and theatrical plays.

Go a step further with school technology – beyond sharing standard details with parents in the school app. Ensure that teachers are posting comments and questions specifically for parents at least once a week for every child, so parents can see and have the opportunity to get more involved in the conversation about their own children.

Top tip: Bring the family together for fun and engagement

Organise family workshops – during and after school, both in person and virtually, to cater for timetables and personal preferences – where you can discuss homework, tests and study skills. Make these events unique and enjoyable: turn 'Mother's days' and 'Father's days' into an opportunity to celebrate matriarchs and patriarchs and how they can respectively make a difference in their child's progress.

Choose venues to help parents and pupils feel relaxed

Consider the feasibility of having school recruitment or new year start events away from the school, in venues where parents may feel more comfortable – for example, sports or community clubs. Use this opportunity to ask someone from within the community – such as a local sports coach, with whom parents might be familiar or feel less threatened – to speak with pupils and parents together about their role in the success of their children.

Chapter 7

Pillar 4: Communication

Area for development: Parents receive simple and easy-to-access information that is clear and consistent

Activity summary:

- Create a school communication calendar for your school team for planned and coordinated parent messages.

- Consider a 'traffic light' approach to ensure that urgent, important and nice-to-know parent information is clearly communicated.

- Create a checklist for good parental communication with standards and guidance.

- Assign responsibility to one person for all parental communication.

Create a school communication calendar

Develop a school communication calendar for your school team that includes all known communication activities with parents. You should be clear about the purpose of every single communication that takes place, no matter how or by whom it is sent. It should be obvious to parents what they should do as a result and how it will impact the learning of their child. Follow these principles to make things simple and easy to access:

- **Why:** Understand the outcome and why you are communicating. This will help you to measure whether you have succeeded.

- **Who:** Be clear about your audience and their concerns and motivations. Different audiences will have different types of knowledge, so avoid assuming information and using acronyms.

● **What:** Ensure that you always put the best interests of pupils at the heart of what you communicate — they are common motivators between school and parents.

● **When:** Plan your activities so you don't send lots of messages on the same day to the same group(s) of parents. Information overload will result in parents either not paying attention or, worse, being frustrated and having a negative reaction. Aim to join up communications where you can to reduce frequency, increase impact, and demonstrate a planned and organised approach.

● **How:** Avoid using the same ways of communicating with parents for everything, whether that is email, a parent app or the school website. The best channel will be dictated by the outcome you want to achieve. Particularly in our post COVID-19 and virtual world, with children receiving more remote education at home, parents have had to adapt, be creative and take a more active role in engaging their children with their schoolwork. Always provide a feedback option for parents.

The calendar could be made available for viewing or editing in a shared online area for anyone within your school community who has to send correspondence en masse. The senior leadership team should review the calendar during a meeting every week, looking at least a week ahead and checking that activities have been completed and understanding the implications of any that have not. The parent communication coordinator should also regularly share updates with the whole school team to remind them to check planned activities before issuing any unplanned parent communications.

Consider a 'traffic light' approach to ensure that information is clearly communicated to parents

For each item in your school communication calendar, categorise whether it is urgent, important or nice to know. You should not have many urgent messages at the planning stage, as these are usually last-minute and unexpected announcements that need to be shared immediately. We recommend that you develop a traffic light system for sharing different levels of messages with parents. This can also provide a common language within the school team. Examples of a school communication plan to manage school messages and a traffic light template are included in Appendix VI.

Top tip: Take a traffic light approach

Use the traffic light colours to establish a common language for your school team so they can be clear about the priority of messages:

Red — urgent and important.

Amber — important but not urgent.

Green — nice to know.

Each colour will have different protocols, including sign-offs, content sections and how they are shared, so parents receive clear communications which they read and action as required.

With your school communication calendar based on known and planned communication activities, you will be in a better position to manage unexpected and urgent messages. For example, if a school team member needs to urgently communicate with a parent group, they can quickly check the communication plan to see what else is planned that day. If there are important or nice-to-know announcements that are not time sensitive, they could be moved on by a day or two to enable the urgent message to be shared, with clear air space from a parent perspective.

If these communications are time sensitive and can't be moved, at least your school team member is aware of what else is planned and has the opportunity to consider whether messages can be combined or consolidated, if appropriate. Either way, it will help to avoid communication overload and demonstrate a planned approach to connecting with parents.

Create a checklist for good parental communication

Create a checklist for parent announcements to help the school team fill out the communication calendar. It should include the following questions:

- Why are we sending this message to parents?
- What do we want them to think, feel and do as a result?
- How important and urgent is the message?
- Are there any other messages that we could combine it with?

- Who needs to sign off or be involved from the school team?
- How will parents receive it/know where to find it?
- How will we know whether parents have received it and understood it?
- What should parents do if they have questions or feedback?
- How will we use this feedback and ensure we respond in a timely way?

Assign responsibility to one person for all parental communication

Ideally, you would nominate a school team member as the parent communication coordinator. This person would maintain oversight of all messages, planned and unplanned. They would be responsible for managing the school communication calendar and keeping it up to date, working with others.

Area for development: The school is focused on listening to parents and pupils

Activity summary:

- Support your regular parent pulse surveys with a more extensive annual survey.
- Choose a measure to identify how likely parents are to recommend your school.
- Use parent events as an opportunity for feedback.
- Ensure parents know you have listened to their feedback and acted where possible.

Listen continuously to parents, supported by an annual parent survey

As mentioned above, good communication is a two-way process, so listen to your parents continuously by adopting a planned listening approach.

Aim to listen to every single parent in school at least once a year. Start by listening to new parents at an individual level to understand their hopes and fears for themselves and their children. This should go beyond a traditional five-minute parent consultation. It should be a more in-depth and structured discussion which sets expectations on both sides and builds foundations for the relationship that is to follow. It should be the point at which the importance of parental support is shared and intentions can be agreed and cemented. Ideally, you would repeat this every year, with teachers having full access to what has been discussed and agreed previously.

You also need to listen collectively by asking for feedback through regularly planned formal initiatives. We recommend that you conduct frequent pulse surveys throughout the year and a fuller parental satisfaction exercise at least once a year. This could be an online survey of all parents or a smaller representative sample. Whichever method you choose, follow up any issues raised through further individual or focus group discussions.

Top tip: How to take a pulse

Pulse surveys enable you to take a rapid check on topics that you want to track regularly over time. They should comprise no more than three to six questions and should be very easy to answer. As the results are quick to review, they can be used to gain an insight into issues that need immediate attention.

Choose a measure to understand your advocates

In your annual parent survey, include a question asking how likely they would be to recommend your school to other parents — a net promoter score. Simply add a question that asks parents to rate how likely they are to recommend your school on a scale of 1 to 10 (where 10 is highly likely and 1 is highly unlikely). If your average score is 9 or above then you have a high number of parents who are 'promoters' and will talk positively about your school to others. If you have an average score of 6 or below, you have a large number of 'detractors' who may talk about your school in a less positive way. If your parental net promoter score is low, then you have work to do on parental engagement.

Use parent events as an opportunity for feedback

Listen informally through instant feedback mechanisms such as quick polls on your website or social media. You can also canvass parents' opinions on the spot via their mobile devices using tools such as Mentimeter (www.mentimeter.com), AhaSlides (https://ahaslides.com) or Vevox (www.vevox.com). Or simply ask parents to complete a paper questionnaire before they leave and drop it into a post box on their way out.

Don't miss an opportunity to gather valuable immediate feedback that will enable you to understand whether your goal has been achieved. Use 'open house' type sessions, where parents have the option to drop into school during agreed times, either in person or online using tools such as Microsoft Teams or Zoom. These are less formal and the outcomes are not going to be representative as the audience is self-selected, but they offer a great chance to hear from parents about topics they want to speak about. If you would rather hold these types of open forums without seeing lots of faces, then host an online discussion using tools such as private chat rooms, where parents type questions and school team members respond.

Ensure parents know you have listened

Whatever your approach to parent feedback, always let parents know they have been heard and what you did or will do as a result. If you couldn't take any action, let parents know why. This builds trust and the belief that the school is listening, thereby enabling the relationship with parents to grow and flourish.

Adopt a listening approach with pupils too. If you have a pupil council, empower them to feed back on topics that are important to them, including parent communication. Ask pupils to facilitate focus groups on specific topics and find out if they can validate the feedback you have gathered from their parents.

Case study: Working with families to achieve the best outcome for children at Specialist Education Services

Specialist Education Services (SES) provide highly specialised, integrated and therapeutic residential care and education for young people from Norfolk, Suffolk, East Anglia and the rest of the UK. They have an outstanding track record in meeting the needs of young people with severe and complex social, emotional and mental health issues, often further complicated by specific learning difficulties. Head of care Dan Baldock and executive principal Neil Dawson explained how they work with and communicate closely with families to achieve amazing results for children.

What was the challenge?

Amy [name changed] was 11 when her parents reached out to SES. She had autism, bipolar disorder and multiple anxiety disorders. She also acted very young for her age. Her parents were both working and were struggling to cope with her behaviour at home, including her relationship with her sibling. Amy couldn't attend mainstream school.

What actions did the SES team take?

When Amy first arrived, the SES team focused on meeting separately with her mum and dad to learn as much as possible about her and the family. They spent time understanding patterns of behaviour, what she had done, what she liked and disliked, what did and didn't work. This understanding was fundamental to ensuring that Amy's journey was successful. Amy's mum's views have been listened to continuously, as the team recognised that she was the expert on her own child.

The SES team — including a case coordinator, personal tutor, link tutor and learning mentor — wrapped themselves around Amy, providing her with full support. Amy also worked with a systemic family therapist and independent child and adolescent psychiatrist. They put a rigid framework in place, especially for family contacts.

However, this was far from a standard off-the-shelf approach. The team shaped everything around Amy's specific personal needs and were highly flexible to adapting the plan as they listened and learned. They planned ahead with her mum, so there was a clear path which was understood by everyone and enabled them to work together towards the same goal. It was important that Amy understood that it wasn't her versus everyone else, but a triangle of people around her who were there to support and care constantly.

Slowly, the team made progress, continuing to work with her parents, particularly Amy's mum. Initially, they had daily conversations with her mum. These moved to weekly over time. The team understood the importance of communication — that they needed to speak with Amy as a united team with her parents, with Amy's interests at the heart of everything.

About the results

Amy is now 16. She is fit and well and, importantly, she is more in tune with what she wants to do with her life, including taking GCSEs. She also likes drama. She has people around her whom she is proud to call her friends. Amy has also undertaken work experience in a children's nursery and would love to pursue this as a career. The team's relationship with Amy's family was fundamental in helping her to make excellent progress, as was their ability to share a little of themselves by demonstrating their human side.

Area for development: School team members are appropriately trained in communicating confidently with parents

Activity summary:

- Prioritise training for school team members so they can communicate with parents with confidence, focusing on:

  ▼ Being prepared to communicate, concentrating on what they want to achieve, who they are communicating with, what they want to communicate and how.

  ▼ Being physically and mentally present so they can observe and connect with their audience.

  ▼ Being open, developing a growth mindset and actively seeking feedback.

  ▼ Being firm but fair, with confident language and posture.

  ▼ Being empathetic and putting themselves in the shoes of others.

  ▼ Being themselves — being authentic and sharing their own stories.

Provide training to ensure your school team are confident communicators

We recommend that school team members undergo communication training to empower them to communicate with confidence. Our 'Communicate with confidence' framework (see https://fit2communicate.com/fourpillarsbook for a one-page summary) outlines the six stages that are set out on the pages that follow: be prepared, be present, be open, be firm but fair, be empathetic and be yourself. While the stages are not sequential, be prepared is naturally the first area to focus on because it must take place in advance of communicating.

Be prepared

The first point in being prepared is to define your outcome. This means having clarity about what you want a communication to achieve. For example, is it to persuade parents to attend an event at school, or to encourage them to do something specific to support their children's learning at home? Whatever outcome is intended, it is helpful to consolidate the message into three key points. If we consider the example of persuading parents to attend an event at school, the three key points might be:

1   Your support is important because it will help your children to achieve their aims.

2   The event will take place on X [date] and last for X hours.

3   For those of you who are able to attend the event, you and your children will receive further support.

There are probably a whole host of other things to tell parents about the event, but consolidating them into three main points forces a clarity of thinking from school that is likely to be more persuasive, and more likely to achieve the outcome, than a random list of wants. (A school message template appears in Appendix VII.)

The next point is to understand your audience. When we work with schools to help them improve how they communicate with parents, we use a behavioural and communication profiling tool called DISC to identify different communication preferences as split across the population (see Extended DISC International, 2015). This can be applied to any individual or group, including parents. The four DISC preferences are dominance (red), influence (yellow), steadiness (green) and conscientiousness (blue). Obviously, it would be impractical to 'profile' each parent, but you can look out for the key indicators of their communication preferences and adapt your style accordingly.

- 10–15% of parents are *red*. They have a dominant personality and are direct and focused on getting to the point quickly. They will say things like: 'When will that happen?' and 'What are you going to do about it?' Communication with them needs to be short, to the point and outcome focused.

- 25–30% of parents are *yellow*. They have an influential personality and are talkative and optimistic. They will say things like: 'I'm sure my child will be fine' and 'Could they work with X to get that done?' Communication with them can go off on tangents, so it needs to stay on topic while also allowing them to share their ideas.

- 30–35% of parents are *green*. They have a steady personality and are considerate and patient. They will say things like: 'How does X feel about that?' and 'How can I help?' Communication with them needs to be slow paced and avoid giving them any surprises in the process.

- 25–30% of parents are *blue*. They have a conscientious personality and are independent and detail focused. They will say things like: 'Could we look at their data from last term/year?' and 'How many more marks do they need?' Communication with them should be structured and avoid questioning their expertise.

Top tip: You don't need to be an expert to benefit from DISC

Your school team members don't need to be communication behaviour experts to use DISC. They simply need to be able to observe and listen to the parents with whom they interact. For example, if you are inviting parents to a school event, consider how you might communicate to appeal to different personality types. To interest parents with a red preference, start your message with a short summary of the key facts which get to the point quickly. For yellow parents, add some visual imagery or wording and a sense of the social and inclusive elements. For the greens, include details of what will be better for those who attend or take part. Finally, for blues, provide details and structure along with where they can find more information and background reading.

The next point is to prepare to adopt a positive mindset throughout the conversation. This takes practice, especially if faced with a wall of negativity. It helps if you know your topic, which means understanding your pupils when speaking with parents about their children. We covered the importance of having a deeper 'get to know each other' discussion with parents and pupils in the development area: 'The school is focused on listening to parents and pupils' (page 118). This would also enable a school team to communicate with confidence by having a better understanding of what to expect from parents and pupils. Parents are more likely to listen and respect expertise if they feel the school team member has a genuine interest in them and cares about and values their children.

Set the focus (or agenda) for the discussion by sending advance information and then taking control of the conversation from the start. Be clear about the topic under discussion and keep to it, while also remaining open to listening as and when appropriate. This is easier if all the facts are at hand, so gathering all of the relevant information is an important part of the preparation stage. Finally, and particularly when expecting a challenging communication, practise relaxation and visualisation techniques as part of the preparation.

Be present

Communicating with confidence requires that you have presence. This starts with physical presence — eye contact, body language and facial expression. It also requires mental presence — listening and asking the right questions to connect with your audience. To do this, speak with them personally as individuals by putting yourself in their shoes and understanding them, their motivations and their concerns. Use compassion and humour if it is appropriate.

It is also important to show a level of vulnerability. While your audience will look to you for valuable advice and inspiration, they also want you to be yourself and not pretend to be a superhero. This means being human, sharing stories that convey some of your fears and concerns and demonstrating how you manage these positively. Share personal stories to bring your message to life for your audience. Finally, use questions positively to incorporate interactivity and to keep their attention by making it a conversation as much as possible.

Look and listen to what is and is not being said. Excellent communicators can read between the spoken words to understand the broader context of the other person, and of their thoughts and needs. The DISC categories we mentioned in the previous section are also important. Red parents will listen better if information is provided in bite-sized chunks with a strong focus on outcomes. Yellows will listen if the conversation is light, engaging and fun, with plenty of opportunities for them to have some input. People who are green will listen if the focus is on people and community and have time to think things through. Blues will listen if they can see a clear structure to the conversation and if supporting evidence is provided or available to them. Ask the right questions to clarify understanding and build rapport that demonstrates a genuine interest. Staying present also means being ready to adapt your approach if the conversation is not going as planned or needs a push in a different direction.

Be open

The key to being open in how you communicate is to maintain a growth mindset. Individuals who believe their talents can be developed — through hard work, good strategies and input from others — have a growth mindset. They tend to achieve more than those with a more fixed mindset, who believe their talents are innate gifts. This is because they worry less about looking smart and put more energy into learning.

When entire companies embrace a growth mindset, their employees report feeling more empowered and committed. They also receive far greater organisational support for collaboration and innovation. In contrast, people at primarily fixed mindset companies report more of only one thing: cheating and deception among employees, presumably to gain an advantage in the talent race (Dweck, 2016). Being open means seeing opportunities for growth and development, rather than considering everything to be fixed and unchangeable. It includes both speaking candidly and being open to different views and responses.

Exercise patience, especially when sharing details with parents. Information should be explained at a pace and level of detail they can understand, avoiding the use of acronyms and school-specific phrases. Share your opinion openly and clearly, even if it is contrary to those with whom you are communicating. This is important because it avoids any sense of hidden agendas.

Actively seek feedback by asking open questions such as, 'What do you think?' rather than yes or no questions. Offer suggestions that parents can build on, making it clear that feedback is welcomed. Repeat back what parents have said to both demonstrate listening and check understanding with them. Encourage positive debate from parents, focusing them on possibilities and opportunities.

Finally, and this is more difficult for more extroverted school team members, think before speaking and avoid saying anything in the moment that may be regretted later.

Be firm but fair

Great communicators use confident language such as 'I believe', 'In my experience' and 'Evidence shows', rather than 'I think'. They take their time and pause, avoiding ums and hesitation and using their voices well, supported by great breathing. They maintain positive body language, avoiding folded arms and closed body stances. They sit up, look alert and engaged, and use their hands in an expressive but natural way.

Knowing your boundaries, both personal and professional, is important when having conversations and managing situations assertively. Choose carefully when to give critical feedback; even if it is actually not negative, it may be taken as such by a parent or colleague. Communicating with confidence is also about knowing when not to share something. Consider the other person's communication preferences and when the best time may be and under what conditions. If necessary, convene another meeting.

Be empathetic

People with empathy are great collaborators and problem-solvers with whom others enjoy working. They include everyone without bias, recognising that every opinion is valid even if it is built on fiction rather than facts (particularly if parents are giving views based on what they have heard from their children rather than what has actually happened). Respecting parents means not talking up or down to them but communicating with them as equals, and remembering that it is a partnership with the aim of supporting their children.

Being culturally sensitive with parents requires additional respect and potentially a deeper understanding, especially if they are from a different culture or have any form of disability. It demands a patient approach and to put yourself in their shoes, particularly when faced with a challenging parent or difficult circumstances. Staying engaged and present by managing your own emotions, even if it is clear the conversation may not be concluded in that session, is also critical.

Be yourself

Being yourself starts with having self-awareness of your own communication style and thus recognising and using your strengths. If you are direct and like to get to the point quickly, you need to be able to do this without creating a negative environment for those who may not favour such a direct style of communication. Communicating with confidence means communicating authentically, staying true to yourself, not trying to be someone else and letting your personality shine.

Case study: Communicating with parents during a crisis

A crisis at a school can come in many forms – from a safeguarding issue, a scathing Ofsted report or a sudden closure. The ability to communicate with parents skilfully is never more relevant than during such an event. When a school is under pressure, the spotlight shines very brightly. Every decision, action and message has the potential to either assuage or further escalate the issue. Just like communicating with parents in general, schools and their leaders are not generally provided with a manual on managing communication during challenging times. And, yet, as we set out in our first book, it is possible to map out an outline process, along with message templates, to support school leaders.

We spoke with Ledbury Primary School head teacher Julie Rees, who in January 2019 went through a devastating crisis when her deputy head teacher tragically lost her life very suddenly in a car accident. After receiving the call notifying her of what had happened, Julie had little time to process the news before she realised that her next task would be to communicate it to the school community. Here is her account of the events and what she did next.

It was a Sunday morning, and I was away from home for the weekend when I received the news. I was absolutely devastated as Jill was also a close friend who had been my deputy for 12 years. Initially, the grief hit me like a tsunami, especially as I had never previously lost anyone in that way. Towards the end of the call, I realised that I would have to share this news, firstly with my colleagues and then the wider community. There was no manual for this kind of situation, so I had to be guided by my experience. I immediately called each member of my leadership team, the chair of governors and the local authority. With over 70 staff and 450 children in our school, and the story being reported on the news, I wanted to make sure people heard the true facts as quickly as possible.

On the way back home, I drafted a letter for parents, which I sent to them by email as soon as I got back. I followed this up with a text message to parents to ask them to check their emails. It was a Sunday and normally Jill would have been on the school gate the following morning, welcoming the children into school. In the letter, I asked parents to inform their children of the tragic news, which felt the most appropriate approach. I subsequently posted a message on social media, once I was happy that everyone at school had been informed. I also called the head teacher at the local secondary school so he could also inform his school community.

I then met with my leadership team in school on that Sunday afternoon. We started to make plans with the children in mind. We decided not to have a school assembly the following day as the grief would have been overwhelming. Instead, we arranged for the children to be in their classes and gave their teachers lots of ideas to support them. We then had a whole school assembly on Tuesday, which was a celebration called 'A Smile for Mrs Evans'.

This logical sequence of communication, through both personal means and a cascade, is one that we would recommend. It demonstrated a remarkable ability to think clearly under devastating circumstances. It also reflects a philosophy that we share with Julie – listen first. By putting ourselves in the position of those with whom we are communicating, we are better able to consider their needs.

In the days that followed, the school became a place of sanctuary for everyone who had known Jill. The staffroom was opened up to parents for them to come in and talk. Along with the school team, they received support from the school's well-being team. The local authority provided an educational psychologist to support the school team and pupils. A memorial book was created for the whole school community. Jill's family were kept informed and involved throughout.

Although, as Julie states, there was no manual available to help her and she was guided by her own experience, there are some logical steps to crisis communications:

1   Gather the facts so that what is shared is accurate from the outset.

2   Inform relevant leaders from the school (school leadership team, chair of governors, trust board, local authority), ideally through a personal call or meeting.

3   Inform leaders of other schools within the local community.

4   Ask school leaders to cascade information to their own teams.

5   Inform parents in writing (and follow up by text if possible).

6   Ask parents to inform their own children.

7   Notify the wider community via social media or a press release to local/ national media outlets.

8   Bring the school team together (physically or virtually) as soon as possible.

9   Provide ongoing support, space and listening for all those affected.

10 Create a form of closure to the crisis.

However, even with a framework in place, it is imperative that school leaders demonstrate empathy, not least through active and deliberate listening. Julie summarises this perfectly:

When managing a challenging situation, head teachers need to display their compassion and vulnerability, as well as their logical and analytical side. This is when a school community needs authentic leadership. It is important to understand the people involved in the situation.

Dealing with a crisis is possibly the ultimate test of any school team member's ability to communicate effectively with parents. While every school and situation is different, the ten steps outlined on page 129 are a good template to follow, along with a large dose of empathy. You can find a crisis communication plan toolkit at: https://fit2communicate.com/fourpillarsbook.

Area for development: The school supports parents to communicate with their children

Activity summary:

- Provide guidelines and checklists to support parents in communicating with their children about school.
- Listen to what parents need in order to support them to create impactful resources and guidance.
- Manage challenging conversations with parents through a clear plan.

Provide guidelines and checklists to support parents

Your school should have basic guidelines, hints, tips or checklists for parents on how they can communicate with their children about school. This should be shared with and explained to parents in a format they can digest and then make use of, whether that is in person, online, in a written document or a combination of all three.

Listen to parents and develop what they need

Use your parent survey to capture their specific requirements, such as support with computer use, core subject knowledge, tutoring or even reading with their children. You will develop an understanding of exactly what sort of individual support is required, which can then be targeted where it is wanted rather than to all parents.

Common areas could be addressed in larger groups offered to all parents, such as a drop-in parent–child communication coffee forum, allowing the school to target parents who need additional support with specific topics or find it more difficult than most to communicate with their children.

Here is an example of some simple hints and tips you could give to parents in your school to use with their children:

● Allow your child to settle down after school before asking them about their day.

● Listen first to see if they voluntarily share information.

● Set aside deliberate time to talk about school.

● Share something about your own day first to start the conversation.

● Ask your child direct questions.

● Review teachers' feedback and what is required together.

● Allow them to be themselves in how they share information.

● Help them to solve issues rather than prescribing solutions.

Manage challenging conversations with parents

Remember that you and your school team are looking after what is most important to parents: their child. However well you communicate, though, there will always be situations when difficult conversations are necessary, especially regarding how they support their child. Below are some tips to prepare for and deal with such events.

● **Put the date in your diary.** Avoid putting off a difficult conversation for another day or so — commit to having the conversation and stick to your plan.

● **Prepare fully for the conversation.** Gather facts and evidence before you start. Who do you need to speak with to gather background information? Consider the type of DISC personality[1] you may be dealing with:

▼ *Red: Direct and assertive (even aggressive)*

These parents say what they want, expect immediate responses and appear very impatient. When your school team spot these characteristics,

---

1   As described on page 123, DISC is a behavioural and communication profiling tool to identify different communication preferences.

they need to be receptive and listen to the parents, get to the point quickly and be brief in their approach. They will benefit from offering suggestions and hints rather than directly taking control.

▼ *Yellow: Calm and friendly*

They talk openly around the concern but do not directly tackle it. They conceal their true feelings and only react when they feel challenged personally. With these parents, it is important to be optimistic and positive. Have an open and friendly conversation and be ready for them to share their perspective.

▼ *Green: Reflective and thoughtful*

They avoid conflict and worry about offending or upsetting others. Their drive is to find a compromise without harming relationships. Be patient, gentle and reassuring with these parents, giving them time to reach a decision. Make it clear that you value their help.

▼ *Blue: Reflective and questioning*

These parents appear to be efficient, rational and ask questions that explore all options. They ask for evidence and avoid conflict. Provide them with the detail they need and ensure your approach is logical and thorough. Give them clear and specific examples and work with them towards a potential solution.

Top tip: Use the GROW model to structure your conversation

The GROW model (or process) is a simple way to support goal-setting and problem-solving. It was developed in the UK and has been used extensively since the 1980s.

Consider how you will structure your conversation using the following questions:

- **Goals:** What would you like us to achieve for your child?
- **Reality:** What is the current situation with your child?
- **Options:** What could we do together to achieve your goals?
- **Will:** What will you do and what will school do?

- **Keep a positive mindset.** Regardless of the parent(s) you are preparing to speak with, keep in mind that they may not remember what you say (exactly) but they will remember how you made them feel. Consider how you can create a positive experience, regardless of the message.

- **Confirm and follow up.** When emotions are involved, facts can be confused. Confirm with the parent what you have agreed in your meeting and give them the opportunity to ask any further questions. Follow up on any agreed actions.

Area for development: Parents are recognised and feel valued for their great work

Activity summary:

- Formally say thank you to parents for their role in supporting their child's learning through an email, text or phone call.

- Encourage your school team to demonstrate how they value the partnership with parents to help their children be at their best — at every opportunity.

Formally say thank you

Create simple ways of formally saying thank you to parents and ensuring that best practice is shared with other parents. When you can see or are made aware that certain parents are doing a great job of supporting their children, send them a thank you message by text, email or a phone call.

Invite parents into school for an informal coffee (or to a virtual meeting) to say thank you to them in person. Or invite them to lunch at the school — perhaps out of sight of their children if that might be too embarrassing for them! If parents are unable to attend school in person or virtually, then arrange to visit them at home instead.

Create a thank you schedule (e.g. one meeting a month) to ensure that it is taken seriously. You could ask your role model parents to speak to other parents at school events, share their achievements with your local media or even publicise it on your own school social media.

Top tip: Make recognition a habit

Make thanking parents a regular habit. We all get busy and even the best intentions can fade away when the pressure of term time hits. Consider putting something in your diary where, for example, every Friday between 9 and 10am you will spend time sending messages or calling parents to thank them for their support for their child. This is particularly important for the school leadership team, but it is a habit that can be adopted by any school team member.

Encourage your school team to demonstrate they value parents

Demonstrating that parents are valued, as part of a partnership with the school, should be part of what every member of the school team does on a daily basis. Make it clear that the parent relationship is critical and that staff are expected to nurture it through continued gratitude. When the school team meets with parents, ensure they thank parents for their support.

Case study: Parent council in a Kent Primary School

Jenny Ross is parent council chair for a Kent primary school. After living in the local community and understanding the needs and requirements of local families, it became apparent that a new initiative to welcome parents into the school was vital. Jenny had previously worked in the local children's centre and understood the needs and concerns of local families, enabling her to appreciate the importance of working collaboratively to close the gap between school and home. Certain circumstances had made this difficult – the school is located within an area of deprivation and had a record of disengaging with families under the previous leadership.

However, with a new head teacher in place, the pupil population rising to almost 350 and its location remaining within 30% of the most deprived neighbourhoods in the country, this seemed the right time to develop the foundations for a new community action group within the school. Encouraging parents back into the school was no easy task, especially for those who were fearful of education from their own days at school. Jenny said, 'For me, this highlighted that educational establishments have a duty of responsibility to support parents and carers, as well as the children they teach.'

After approval by the head teacher and school governors, the council began to take shape. As it developed, so did its success and impact within the school. Formal meetings took place every six weeks and other events were held in-between meetings. The council was beginning to support the local community and contribute to the wider issues in the school through policy and practice decisions.

Relationships with food banks, the local community centre, church groups and wildlife conservation trusts provided vital links with the wider community, offering advice, guidance and training for families during challenging times. From very small and humble beginnings, the council grew to over 20 representatives across 14 classrooms. This included a chair, two administrators and the backing of the head teacher.

Jenny said, 'Our success did not come without barriers. At the beginning of the process we had to gain trust and try to reduce the feeling of suspicion. The need for equality was one of the main focuses – some parents were concerned they would be attending a meeting "to be talked at" rather than contribute to. The definition of roles, the balance in equality, trust and fair ownership all helped contribute to a group that now feels empowered and able to play their part in the educational experience of the local community.'

Final Thoughts

Throughout this book, we have focused on the importance of the relationship between school, parents and pupils in achieving active parental engagement, using a listen first approach and the framework of the four pillars of knowledge, environment, culture and communication. Giving pupils a voice at school is not new or innovative, and nor is listening to parents to understand their concerns and how to best support them. Aiming to share knowledge about why positive parental engagement matters, creating an environment in which it is supported and a culture in which it can flourish, and developing communication habits that make it happen may also appear as obvious and desirable things to do. The four pillars are not overly onerous or difficult to implement. And yet, active parental engagement remains a challenge for many of the schools we work with or simply hear from. It is a problem they will openly acknowledge, but tend to implement only temporary solutions in order to tackle it.

Although we do not consider the approach described in this book to be new, we do believe that looking at the challenge of active parental engagement through these lenses of the four pillars offers a clarity that has never before been available to school leaders. Any school can adopt the simple framework of the four pillars of active parental engagement, regardless of location, demographic or status. They offer a consistency of approach and are supported by research and science.

A lack of consistency is often the biggest barrier for schools trying to address the problem of active parental engagement. Some have undertaken one or more of the four pillars in isolation, and either given up or changed approach before achieving their objective. Intuitively, schools know that, together, knowledge, environment, culture and communication can create a powerful approach to parental engagement, but they haven't sufficiently thought through what success will look like practically. We hope that our model inspires positive change which results in successful outcomes for schools, parents and pupils.

Making it happen

The ongoing challenge for schools is to blend the prescribed school learning experience with the needs and demands of the real world and the hopes and dreams of a generation. Or, to put it another way, to bring knowledge, environment, culture and communication together to create an engaging experience.

As described in Chapters 3–7, we recommend a structured and systematic approach to implementing the four pillars of active parental engagement. Unlike flicking to the end of a book to find out the conclusion, there is no shortcut to active parental engagement. It has to be deeply embedded in the school strategy with specific and measurable goals to define success. Every successful small step forwards must be noted and celebrated to provide the necessary energy to continue to drive forwards what can sometimes feel like a thankless task. Self-evaluating the starting point is critical to understanding where to focus limited time and resources. Understanding which of the four pillars requires the most attention will provide a basis for action and define how much emphasis to give to each one.

The opportunity — and the threat — for every school is that nothing stands still. The very nature of schooling means that at the end of every school year approximately 20% of pupils will leave and their parents will cease to be targets for active parental engagement. At the same time, new pupils will join, bringing with them new parents who will become fresh targets for active parental engagement. This cyclical turnover means that active parental engagement is never done, which means continually reviewing, planning, evaluating and, importantly, listening. New parents bring the hopes of the next generation, along with new concerns and challenges but also new opportunities. We believe that active parental engagement should be given the same status and rigour as the annual budgeting process.

What next?

As technology advances and the future of work continues to shift, especially in the wake of the COVID-19 pandemic, so will the four pillars model. For example, the online environment we describe will certainly continue to evolve. What might be considered forward thinking in 2021 may be normal practice in just a few years' time, so we remain focused on ensuring that the 20 outcomes we have defined are the right ones to achieve active parental engagement across all schools.

The speed of change has already intensified. For example, the unimaginably rapid roll-out of remote collaboration technology (such as Teams) during the coronavirus lockdowns demonstrates that schools, parents and pupils can and will adapt to change. This upheaval has opened up opportunities for flipped learning and greater parental engagement. With tutors more able to engage directly with pupils and their parents through the direct link to home via the internet, they can offer one-to-one support and mentoring, and help expand on knowledge learned outside the classroom.

There is a real opportunity for schools to make use of technology in ways that empower parents, respect their personal circumstances and develop trusting relationships that ultimately benefit their children. In our own research with parents, we have heard comments on communication and engagement that are as positive as, 'I love my son's school and we have a great relationship to support my son's learning', and as negative as, 'I just feel they give you a lot of communication through technology, but I've barely spoken 10 words to my daughter's new Year 3 teacher and I didn't speak with the previous teacher either.'

Further research

We would also like to see more and much wider research in the field of parental engagement than has been possible within the scope of this book, focusing, in particular, on the generational differences between the parents of tomorrow compared to the parents of today. Those children born in the early 2020s, who will be targets for active parental engagement around 2050, are likely to have different perspectives and expectations of their role in the school–pupil–parent relationship. Schools may not even exist in the way they do today, but pupils will still need the support of their parents to ensure they are able to learn and grow, alongside whatever education looks like in the middle of the 21st century.

Appendix I:

The Four Pillars of Parental Engagement

Four pillars of parental engagement

A step-by-step framework for schools to ensure pupils can be at their best.

Knowledge

✔ Parents, school team and pupils **know what is expected** of them in the partnership.

✔ Parents know **why, when and how to support** their children's learning.

✔ Parents are **able to use school technology**, including portals, apps and tools.

✔ Parents know how to access and understand their **children's progress information**.

✔ Parents know **whom to contact for help** and when they can expect a response.

Environment

✔ The school team create a school **environment that welcomes** and supports parents.

✔ Parents understand what a **home environment** that supports learning looks like and are supported in creating this.

✔ The school creates an **online environment** where parents find what they need easily.

✔ Parents are encouraged to share their school experiences to **support continuous improvement and learning**.

✔ The school and parents **respect time** commitments.

Culture

✓ School leaders build a **planned school culture** that supports parents, pupils and the school.

✓ The school supports the building of **trusted relationships** between the school team, parents and pupils.

✓ The school team understands and **respects parents' beliefs**, culture, expectations and parenting style.

✓ The school supports **parental involvement** in initiatives and bodies.

✓ The school **involves pupils and parents together**.

Communication

✓ Parents receive **simple and easy-to-access information** that is clear and consistent.

✓ The school is focused on listening to **parents and pupils**.

✓ School team members are appropriately **trained in communicating confidently** with parents.

✓ The school supports parents to **communicate with their children**.

✓ Parents are **recognised and feel valued** for their great work.

Appendix II:

Parent Promise Workshop Guide

This workshop guide will help your school team members to co-create your parent promise. You should include a range of people from your school team with different perspectives and roles.

Before the workshop

Understand current perceptions

Prior to your workshop, use research to understand the current perceptions of the school team, pupils and parents. You can do this in various ways:

- Review what current and prospective parents are saying about your school online, such as Netmums (www.netmums.com).

- Refer to the results of parent surveys or consider running a short pulse survey.

- Refer to the school team research and any insights related to their relationships and ability to engage with parents.

- Refer to feedback from pupils and how they believe your school supports parents.

During the workshop

Be clear about what you want to achieve

Start your workshop by sharing what you want to achieve — that is, define your school's parent promise. Then share the findings from your research, including positive and less positive comments and insights about how you currently engage with parents.

Understand where your school wants to be — your parent promise

Ask everyone what they would like the parent promise to be. It should be simple, credible, memorable and inspiring. It should also help you to connect with parent 'customers' in terms of what makes your school different, and it should echo your purpose and values.

Consider:

- What makes your school special — your 'secret sauce'?
- How would you like your school to be talked about?
- Is there anything that stands in your way?
- What can you learn from the past?

An example parent promise could be: *We are passionate about empowering pupils to be at their best so they can make a positive difference and shape a better world.*

Develop proof points

Once you have a draft parent promise, think about what proof points you have to support it — that is, where and how you are already doing this. For example, if you want pupils to make a difference and create a better world, you might already offer them the opportunity to work with charities and on community projects. Your promise can also be slightly aspirational in terms of what you want to achieve in the future.

Develop a plan to deliver on your promise

Consider those moments that matter from the point of view of parents (e.g. when they first visit school with their child, the child's first day at school). Identify from your research how you can improve parents' experience at these junctures with specific actions supported by the four pillars model of knowledge, environment, culture and communication.

After the workshop

Agree the promise and create a plan of action

After your workshop, share the promise with relevant members of your senior leadership team who were not involved in the workshop. Ensure it is agreed on by all.

Ideally, test the parent promise with some friendly parents. Ask for their reactions: is it clear? Is it positive? Is it something they believe the school delivers on?

Now share it with your broader school team and make sure they understand what it means for them. Identify actions that will ensure the promise is met in terms of what parents experience. Agreed actions should have a clear owner and deadline, and the senior leadership team should intervene when things aren't happening as they should.

Review how you are doing in delivering your parent promise

Delivering your parent promise needs to happen consistently in order to build trust and create experiences that parents talk about positively to others. Continue to ask for feedback and carry out short surveys to ensure that you are fulfilling and even surpassing expectations.

Appendix III:

Parental Engagement Activity Template

Use this template to share and track the actions you need to take as a team to deliver your parental engagement strategy. This should be reviewed regularly and progress shared with the senior leadership team. It will also enable the school team to be aware of any delays or escalating issues that may be getting in the way of delivery. Make the plan available in a shared online place, so you can work jointly to achieve your parental engagement goals.

Activity start date	Activity end date	Audience	Activity detail	Outcome	Owner	Sign-off	Status/ notes
		e.g. School team	e.g. Training in communicating with parents	e.g. Build confidence of school team in communicating well with parents			

Appendix IV:

School Information Finder

Identify the questions that parents ask most often and add them to the column on the left (we have included some examples below). You can then provide up-to-date information on the right, so parents can find what they need quickly, whether it is available on your website or the parent portal. Aim to include direct links wherever you can. This information finder can be shared online.

What information do you need?	Where to find the information
I need to contact the school urgently.	e.g. Phone the school office during school hours or email: urgent@school name.com.
I need to contact the school for a non-urgent matter.	
I need to find a list of teachers.	
I need to know the term dates.	
I need to see if my child has any homework.	
I want an update on my child's progress.	
I want to report my child as too sick to attend school.	
I want to find out about school trips.	

Appendix V:

School Communication Calendar

It is important to have a clear view of what communications are planned, and when, so you don't overload anyone in your school community and to ensure that important messages are not lost. This plan will also help you to manage last-minute messages as you will be able to see quickly if there are any clashes or what might need to be rearranged as a result. The example below will support you to create your own.

When	Recipient	What	How	Communicator
XX	All school team	Parents' evening update	Email	Head teacher
XX	Year 7 parents	Internet safety talk	Email with link to parent portal	Head of Year 7
XX	All parents	New data protection rules	Email with link to parent portal	Head of IT
XX	Local media	Pupils selected to represent GB sports team	Media release and phone calls	Deputy head
XX	All school team	New rules for visitors	Leaflet/poster in staffroom	School office manager
XX	Year 9 parents	Options evening	Teams event	Head of Year 9

Appendix VI:

A Traffic Light Approach to Managing Information

Help your team to understand how to prioritise your school information using this simple traffic light approach. This will ensure a better response from your school community and save time chasing actions.

Always specify what action is required and by when, or whether the message is for information only.

Add a contact for further information in case there are questions.

| Red
Urgent and important | Amber
Important but not urgent | Green
For information |
|---|---|---|
| Example messages:

● School closure.

● Child safety issue. | Example messages:

● Changes to term dates.

● School trip. | Example messages:

● School family day.

● School uniform sale. |
| Governance:

● Requires sign-off by head or deputy head. | Governance:

● Requires sign-off by an appropriate leader. | Governance:

● No sign-off needed but refer to communication principles. |
| Process:

● Send one to three key points by text.

● Consider email follow-up with a read receipt to check the message has been received. | Process:

● Send one to three key points by email. | Process:

● Post one to three key points on website. |

Appendix VII:

Prepare Your School Message

Use the questions below to develop strong messages that will help you to achieve your school communication outcomes.

Your communication outcome	Why and what are you communicating? What is the outcome you want to achieve?
Be audience focused	Who are they? What do you know about them? What do you want them to think, feel and do? How can you communicate inclusively?
Manage the environment/ channel	What is the best way to communicate to support your outcomes? How can you create the right environment?
Introducing your message	How will your capture your audience's attention?
Your top points (up to three)	What are your key points (with supporting evidence)?
How you will close	Aim to repeat the main points and share your call to action.

Bibliography

Action for Children (2019). Childhood in Crisis (9 July) [press release]. Available at: https://www.actionforchildren.org.uk/media-centre/childhood-in-crisis.

American Psychological Association (2012). APA Survey Finds Feeling Valued at Work Linked to Well-Being and Performance (March) [press release]. Available at: https://www.apa.org/news/press/releases/2012/03/well-being.

Aspire (2019). Exam Results: Recruiters Have Their Say (1 July) [press release]. Available at: https://www.aspirejobs.co.uk/news/exam-results-recruiters-have-their-say.

Bright Horizons and Working Families (2019). *Modern Families Index 2019*. Available at: https://workingfamilies.org.uk/wp-content/uploads/2019/02/BH_MFI_Report_2019_Full-Report_Final.pdf.

British Muslims for Secular Democracy (2010). *Advice for Schools: Brief Guidance for Handling Muslim Parental Concern*. Available at: https://www.ed.ac.uk/files/atoms/files//schools.pdf.

Cosgrove, J. B. (2018). Why Getting Enough Parent Volunteers is Harder Than Ever and How You Can Still Succeed, *School Volunteers Share* (6 September) [blog]. Available at: https://www.schoolvolunteersshare.com/blog/2018/9/5/volunteer-recruiting-fixes.

Cuff, M. (2020). More Than Half of Child Psychiatrists Are Seeing Patients with Eco-Anxiety, *The i* (20 November). Available at: https://inews.co.uk/inews-lifestyle/wellbeing/child-psychiatrists-patients-eco-anxiety-climate-crisis-765882.

Daniel, G. (2015). Patterns of Parent Involvement: A Longitudinal Analysis of Family–School Partnerships in the Early Years of School in Australia, *Australasian Journal of Early Childhood*, 40(1): 119–128. Available at: https://www.researchgate.net/publication/275837365_Patterns_of_Parent_Involvement_A_Longitudinal_Analysis_of_Family-School_Partnerships_in_the_Early_Years_of_School_in_Australia/link/5b420552a6fdccbcf90b8105/download.

Dempster, K. and Robbins, J. (2017). *Build Communication Success in Your School: A Guide for School Leaders* (Abingdon: Routledge).

Department for Education (2019). *Teacher Appraisal and Capability: A Model Policy for Schools*. Available at: https://assets.publishing.service.gov.uk/government/uploads/system/uploads/attachment_data/file/786143/Teacher_appraisal_and_capability-model_policy.pdf.

Desforges, C. and Abouchaa, A. (2003). *The Impact of Parental Involvement, Parental Support and Family Education on Pupil Achievement and Adjustment* (Nottingham: Department for Education and Skills). Available at: https://dera.ioe.ac.uk/6305/1/rr433.pdf.

Dufur, M. J., Parcel, T. L. and Troutman, K. P. (2013). Does Capital at Home Matter More Than Capital at School? Social Capital Effects on Academic Achievement, *Research in Social Stratification and Mobility*, 31: 1–21. Available at: https://cdn.chass.ncsu.edu/sites/socant.chass.ncsu.edu/documents/Parcel_3.pdf.

Dweck, C. (2016). What Having a 'Growth Mindset' Actually Means, *Harvard Business Review* (13 January). Available at: https://hbr.org/2016/01/what-having-a-growth-mindset-actually-means.

Education Endowment Foundation (2018). Families and Schools Together (FAST): Evaluation Report and Executive Summary (November). Available at: https://educationendowmentfoundation.org.uk/public/files/Projects/Evaluation_Reports/FAST.pdf.

Extended DISC International (2015). *Extended DISC Personal Analysis: Validation Report*. Available at: https://www.one4.eu/blog/wp-content/uploads/2017/05/Extended-DISC-Validation-Report-2015_client.pdf.

Friedrich, A., Flunger, B., Nagengast, B., Jonkmann, K. and Trautwein, U. (2015). Pygmalion Effects in the Classroom: Teacher Expectancy Effects on Students' Math Achievement, *Contemporary Educational Psychology*, 41: 1–12.

Glazzard, J. and Rose, A. (2019). *The Impact of Teacher Wellbeing and Mental Health on Pupil Progress in Primary Schools*. Available at: https://www.leedsbeckett.ac.uk/carnegie-school-of-education/research/carnegie-centre-of-excellence-for-mental-health-in-schools/school-mental-health-network/-/media/253bcf64213a4a8582a2a0a2be6b1d49.ashx.

Graham, H. (2017). Bad Teenage Experiences Scare Parents Away from Their Child's School – But Heads Want to Change That, *Chronicle Live* (30 October). Available at: https://www.chroniclelive.co.uk/news/north-east-news/bad-teenage-experiences-scare-parents-13827626.

Hattie, J. (2008). *Visible Learning: A Synthesis of Over 800 Meta-Analyses Relating to Achievement*, 1st edn (Abingdon and New York: Routledge).

Holloman, H. and Yates, P. H. (2013). Cloudy with a Chance of Sarcasm or Sunny with High Expectations: Using Best Practice Language to Strengthen Positive Behavior Intervention and Support Efforts, *Journal of Positive Behavior Interventions*, 15(2): 124–127.

Humphrey, C. and Macdonald, E. (2018). Why a People-Centred Culture is Crucial in the Digital Age, *Reuters Events* (30 July). Available at: https://www.reutersevents.com/sustainability/why-people-centred-culture-crucial-digital-age.

Issimdar, M. (2018). Homeschooling in the UK Increases 40% Over Three Years, *BBC News* (25 April). Available at: https://www.bbc.co.uk/news/uk-england-42624220.

Lynch, S. and Worth, J. (2017). More Teachers Are Joining Than Leaving the Profession, But Will It Be Enough to Meet Demand? *National Foundation for Educational Research* (22 June) [blog]. Available at: https://www.nfer.ac.uk/news-events/nfer-blogs/more-teachers-are-joining-than-leaving-the-profession-but-will-it-be-enough-to-meet-demand.

National Association of School Business Management (NASBM) (2016). Engaging Parents and Other Stakeholders to Improve Your School. Available at: https://isbl.org.uk/PublicDocuments/105224.2416577Engaging%20Parents%20and%20Stakeholder%20Effectively%20Final.pdf.

Nicola (2017). Reading Aloud: Giving Children the Best Start, *Minds of Wonder* (11 January) [blog]. Available at: https://mindsofwonder.com/2017/01/11/reading-aloud-giving-children-the-best-start.

McDonald, L., Moberg, D. P., Brown, R., Rodriguez-Espiricueta, I., Flores, N. I., Burke, M. P. and Coover, G. (2006). After-School Multifamily Groups: A Randomized Controlled Trial Involving Low-Income, Urban, Latino Children. *Children & Schools*, 28(1), 25–34.

Mann, C. R. (1918). *A Study of Engineering Education. Prepared for the Joint Committee on Engineering Education of the National Engineering Societies* (Boston, MA: Merrymount Press). Available at: https://www.nationalsoftskills.org/downloads/Mann-1918-Study_of_Engineering_Educ.pdf.

Mohsin, M. (2020). 10 Email Marketing Statistics That You Need to Know in 2021, *Oberlo* (1 June). Available at: https://www.oberlo.co.uk/blog/email-marketing-statistics.

Molnar, M. (2012). Study: Parents More Influential Than Schools in Academic Success, *Education Week* (10 October). Available at: https://www.edweek.org/education/study-parents-more-influential-than-schools-in-academic-success/2012/10.

Ofsted (2018). *The Annual Report of Her Majesty's Chief Inspector of Education, Children's Services and Skills 2017/18*. Available at: https://assets.publishing.service.gov.uk/government/uploads/system/uploads/attachment_data/file/761606/29523_Ofsted_Annual_Report_2017-18_041218.pdf.

Poorkavoos, M. (2016). Eight Behaviours That Build Trust, *Roffey Park Institute* (19 October). Available at: https://www.roffeypark.ac.uk/knowledge-and-learning-resources-hub/eight-behaviours-that-build-trust.

Save the Children (2020). Families and Schools Together. Available at: https://www.savethechildren.org.uk/what-we-do/uk-work/in-schools/fast.

Schwab, K. (2016). The Fourth Industrial Revolution: What It Means, How To Respond, *World Economic Forum* (14 January). Available at: https://www.weforum.org/agenda/2016/01/the-fourth-industrial-revolution-what-it-means-and-how-to-respond.

Sénéchal, M. and Young, L. (2008). The Effect of Family Literacy Interventions on Children's Acquisition of Reading from Kindergarten to Grade 3: A Meta-Analytic Review, *Review of Educational Research*, 78(4): 880–907.

Sinek, S. (2011). *Start with Why: How Great Leaders Inspire Everyone to Take Action* (London: Penguin).

UKEssays (2018). How Does Culture Affect Parenting Styles? Available at: https://www.ukessays.com/essays/education/parenting-styles-the-influence-of-ethnicity-and-culture-education-essay.php?vref=1.

University of Missouri (2017). Students More Likely to Succeed if Teachers Have Positive Perceptions of Parents (20 February) [press release]. Available at: https://munewsarchives.missouri.edu/news-releases/2017/0220-students-more-likely-to-succeed-if-teachers-have-positive-perceptions-of-parents.

van Poortvliet, M., Axford, N. and Lloyd, J. (2019). *Working with Parents to Support Children's Learning: Guidance Report*. Available at: https://educationendowmentfoundation.org.uk/public/files/Publications/ParentalEngagement/EEF_Parental_Engagement_Guidance_Report.pdf.

World Economic Forum (2018). *Towards a Reskilling Revolution: A Future of Jobs for All*. Available at: http://www3.weforum.org/docs/WEF_FOW_Reskilling_Revolution.pdf.

World Economic Forum (2020). *Resetting the Future of Work Agenda: Disruption and Renewal in a Post-COVID World. White Paper*. Available at: http://www3.weforum.org/docs/WEF_NES_Resetting_FOW_Agenda_2020.pdf.

World Economic Forum (2020). *The Future of Jobs Report 2020*. Available at: http://www3.weforum.org/docs/WEF_Future_of_Jobs_2020.pdf.